I0825039

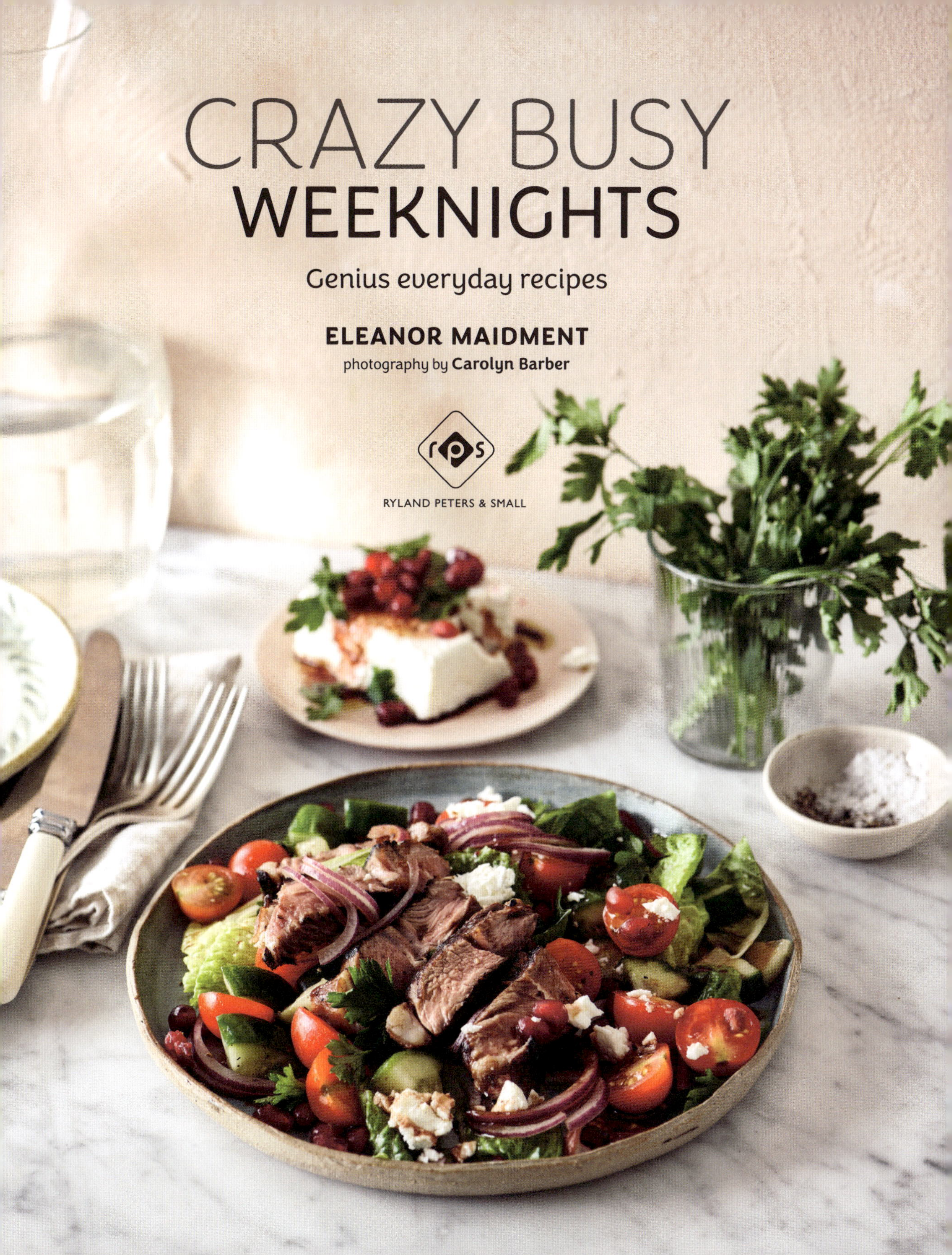

CRAZY BUSY WEEKNIGHTS

Genius everyday recipes

ELEANOR MAIDMENT

photography by **Carolyn Barber**

rps

RYLAND PETERS & SMALL

Dedication
This book is dedicated to you, Mum.

Senior Designer Toni Kay
Editorial Director Julia Charles
Creative Director Leslie Harrington
Production Director Patricia Harrington
Indexer Vanessa Bird
Food Stylist Kathy Kordalis
Prop Stylist Hannah Wilkinson

First published in 2026 by
Ryland Peters & Small
20–21 Jockey's Fields
London WC1R 4BW
and
1452 Davis Bugg Road,
Warrenton, NC 27589

www.rylandpeters.com
email:
euregulations@rylandpeters.com

10 9 8 7 6 5 4 3 2 1

ISBN: 978-1-78879-752-8

Printed in China.

A CIP record for this book is available from the British Library.
US Library of Congress Cataloging-in-Publication Data has been applied for.

The authorised representative in the EEA is Authorised Rep Compliance Ltd., Ground Floor, 71 Lower Baggot Street, Dublin, D02 P593, Ireland
www.arccompliance.com

NOTES

- Both British (Metric) and American (Imperial plus US cups) measurements are included in these recipes for your convenience; however it is important to work with only one set of measurements and not alternate between the two within a recipe.
- All spoon measurements are level unless otherwise specified.
- All eggs are medium (UK) or large (US), unless specified as large, in which case US extra-large should be used. Uncooked or partially cooked eggs should not be served to the very old, frail, young children, pregnant women or those with compromised immune systems.
- Ovens should be preheated to the specified temperatures. We recommend using an oven thermometer.
- When a recipe calls for the grated zest of citrus fruit, buy unwaxed fruit and wash well before using. If you can only find treated fruit, scrub well in warm soapy water before using.

CONTENTS

INTRODUCTION

Modern life is busy. No matter who I speak to, or whatever stage of life they're in, everyone seems to be cramming a whole lot into their days. Whether it's work or study, school runs, long commutes, exercise classes, dog walks, or making time to catch up with friends and family, it feels like there's very little energy for anything else. Unfortunately, that often includes cooking and feeding ourselves well, especially during the week. And that is exactly why I wanted to write this book: to show that weeknight cooking can be quick, easy... and highly impressive.

It is often said that the average person has a repertoire of seven meals that they cook on rotation. Recipes that they know by heart, shop for from memory and can prepare on autopilot. Which makes sense in these crazy busy times, because it means there is one less thing to think about. But where's the joy in that? We all need fresh ideas and inspiration, and to experience new flavours and techniques – and that's where this book comes in. Whether it's a super-simple five-ingredient meal, a flavour-packed plate that can be on the table in under 20 minutes or a one-pot wonder that keeps washing up to a minimum, I have covered all of the most common weeknight requirements.

In over 15 years of recipe writing for magazines and newspapers, I have learned that realistic cooking is what people need during the week. That means ingredients readily available from the supermarket (no hunting down obscure sauces and spices), minimal prep times, and simple techniques using only the regular pots and pans you already have at home. But let me be clear: realistic doesn't mean boring. In fact, I think that all of the recipes in this book are actually a masterclass in how to coax the most out of everyday ingredients and unfussy cooking methods.

I passionately believe that we should all be cooking more from scratch and relying less on processed or ready-made meals. In fact, just as I finished writing the final recipes for this book, I began a five-year bachelor's degree in Nutritional Therapy, with the end goal of working with people to optimize their health through food. While I believe strongly in personalized nutrition and that there is no one-size-fits-all answer, I do think the best place to start is knowing how to cook for yourself and using good-quality, unprocessed ingredients.

When creating recipes, I strive to consider all aspects of a dish. I aim for at least one portion of vegetables in the meal (often many more), and try to provide a balance of protein, carbohydrate, fats and fibre. I consider colour and how the food will look on the plate, because we enjoy food more when it looks good. Plus, there's such satisfaction in creating a meal that looks beautiful. I think about textures and including ingredients that we might not always use, because diversity is so important in our diets. I hope this care comes through in the recipes. They are intended to be one-stop meals – easy to make, easy to repeat and a joy to eat.

And with that, I hope I've finally answered the eternal question of 'What shall I have for dinner tonight?'

Eleanor

How to be a great weeknight cook

In my many years of recipe writing, I have come to learn that people consume recipes in different ways. Some are fastidious cooks who follow instructions to the letter (as a recipe writer, I appreciate you!). Others will always make substitutions and tweaks as they see fit, and then there are those who use recipes as pure inspiration, glancing at them before going off to create something entirely of their own.

Regardless of your recipe 'personality type', I hope this book provides an abundance of inspiration for your weeknight cooking. It's a tough gig coming up with fresh ideas week in week out, and my aim here is to provide simple, practical solutions to the eternal conundrum of 'what shall I cook tonight?'

I have tried to make the recipes as accessible and straightforward as possible, with clear and detailed instructions. But cooking is far from an exact science. Ingredients can vary wildly, ovens don't always run true to temperature and equipment like pans and blenders can perform very differently. So, my biggest piece of advice when following these recipes is to go with your instincts.

Your eyes, nose, hands and ears are your greatest tools in the kitchen. When something in the oven smells ready, it probably is. Gently pressing on a steak, chicken breast, or salmon fillet will give you a sense of how well it is cooked. And don't forget to listen, too: onions will hiss if the oil's too hot, but sizzle gently when it's at just the right temperature. These cues are more reliable than any timer.

On a more practical level, here are a few things to keep in mind as you cook from this book:

Ingredients As I've previously mentioned, the ingredients you buy at any given time can vary... a lot. Vegetables can be sweet and soft one month, then dry or bitter the next. Different brands of condiments and spice mixes will have distinct flavour profiles. Even the same type of grain can cook at different rates depending on the batch. Recipes cannot account for every nuance, so taste, adjust, and stay flexible.

Timings Cooking times are a guide, not a rule. You might find that onions take a little longer to brown than suggested, or a sauce has reduced to a good consistency sooner than expected. Use your judgement. Don't be afraid to cook things for longer if they need it. Alternatively, if the cooking process has moved too fast, then perhaps you'll need to add a splash of water to loosen a sauce.

Salt & seasoning Great seasoning is what elevates a dish from good to unforgettable. Salt is the most important seasoning, and often I give measurements to establish a good base level, but it's still worth tasting as you go. Season gradually and at the end ask yourself: 'What does this need for balance?' Perhaps a touch more salt, although bear in mind that it isn't the only seasoning. A squeeze of lemon juice is highly effective at prising out flavour, and a little sugar can balance acidic or savoury notes. And remember that around the world, all sorts of ingredients are used to boost flavour – toasted sesame oil, citrus zest, chilli/hot red pepper flakes, salty cheeses, pomegranate seeds and toasted cumin seeds are all just waiting to illuminate dishes.

Meat, fish & poultry I know weeknight cooking can be time-limited, but ideally meat, fish and poultry shouldn't go straight from fridge to pan. If time allows, take them out 30 minutes (20 minutes for fish) before cooking and season with salt. This will enhance flavour and allow for a more even cook.

Oils In general, I like to fry/sauté with a light olive oil and use a good-quality extra virgin olive oil for dressings and drizzling. If you prefer to cook with vegetable, rapeseed or sunflower oils, then do so, because it won't make much difference to the finished dish.

Stocks Unless cooking for vegetarians, I like to use chicken stock. Be choosy about it, because there's a lot of bad stock available out there. Always look at the ingredients list and avoid those that are high in salt and artificial flavourings. I'm a big fan of bone broths (Borough Broth and Freja are great), which are more expensive but offer excellent quality.

The storecupboard A well-stocked storecupboard is a lifesaver on weeknights. Ingredients like soy sauce, tomato purée/paste, capers and mustards are powerful flavour enhancers, while jars or cans of lentils and beans offer quick, protein-packed solutions. Your spice drawer needn't be extensive, just a handful of essentials – turmeric, cumin, paprika, curry powder – can transform weeknight cooking.

The freezer Like a good kitchen storecupboard, freezers are a secret weapon for weeknight cooking. My own is full of leftover soups and stews, weighed out into portions and neatly stacked for emergency meals. There are also plenty of pre-prepared frozen vegetables, dumplings, falafel, stocks and prawns/shrimp for last-minute dinners.

Ovens All recipes were tested in my home oven using a fan setting. Fan ovens typically run 20°C/68°F hotter than conventional ones, but the truth is that all ovens operate slightly differently, regardless of what temperature is showing on the dial. Some run hot, others cool. Get to know yours and adjust accordingly.

Pots & pans Invest in a few good-quality saucepans and casseroles/Dutch ovens with lids. If you look after them, they will last a long time. I find my most useful pans for weeknight cooking are two ovenproof sauté pans (26 cm/10½ inch and 30 cm/12 inch) with tight-fitting lids, which can be used for frying and simmering, and can go from the hob/stovetop straight into the oven.

Knives You don't need a full knife set. I'd go so far as to say that one good-quality (and regularly sharpened) 18-cm/7-inch or 20-cm/8-inch chef's knife, one smaller serrated knife for cutting things like tomatoes and fresh chillies/chiles and a good bread knife will cover pretty much everything.

Spoon measurements Tablespoons (15 ml) and teaspoons (5 ml) are specific measurements, and regular cutlery spoons won't give the same accuracy. Unless specified as 'heaped' or 'scant', spoon measures given in these recipes are level.

Plant points Finally, a note on plant points, which you will find are given in the Packed with Plants chapter. You will no doubt have heard the chatter about how eating '30 plants a week' is important for the diversity of our gut microbiomes and therefore for our overall health, and I do agree this is a good way to eat. Here, plant points have been calculated according to Zoe guidelines (www.Zoe.com), giving one plant point for each distinct plant variety and ¼ point for items such as herbs and spices. It is, however, like most things related to cooking, not an exact science!

NO COOKING REQUIRED

FRESH, VIBRANT PLATES WITH NOT A POT OR A PAN IN SIGHT.

CHICKEN & CUCUMBER SALAD WITH CHILLI CRISP

A rotisserie chicken is the ultimate convenience food. Here it is zhuzhed up with chilli crisp and served tossed with a smashed cucumber salad, for a punchy supper in no time. This can easily be doubled to feed four.

SMASHED CUCUMBER
2 tbsp light soy sauce
1 tbsp rice vinegar
1 small garlic clove, finely grated
1 tsp toasted sesame oil
½ cucumber

SHREDDED CHICKEN
3 tbsp mayonnaise
1 tsp chiu chow chilli oil (or other chilli crisp), plus extra to serve
½ rotisserie chicken (or about 250 g/9 oz. cooked chicken)

TO SERVE (OPTIONAL)
cooked noodles
black sesame seeds
coriander/cilantro leaves

SERVES 2

TAKES 20 MINUTES

Start by making the smashed cucumber. Mix the soy sauce, vinegar, garlic and sesame oil in a mixing bowl.

Place the cucumber on a chopping board and whack it all over with a rolling pin. (This creates crevices for the dressing to soak into.) Roughly chop the cucumber and stir into the dressing. Set aside.

In a separate mixing bowl, mix the mayonnaise with the chiu chow chilli oil. Remember that these can both vary wildly in heat levels, so you may want to add more or less here, tasting as you go. Shred the chicken and finely chop the skin, then stir into the mayonnaise.

Tip the cucumber and dressing over the chicken, toss everything together and serve. You can eat this as is, or sometimes I pile it over noodles, scattering with black sesame seeds and more chilli oil. Some chopped coriander leaves go nicely, too.

HOT SMOKED TROUT PÂTÉ WITH PICKLED RADISHES

Smoked fish pâtés are such a simple pleasure, they take minutes to make yet feel substantial. You can easily swap the trout for hot smoked salmon, mackerel or even kippers.

160 g/6 oz. hot smoked trout, any skin removed
80 g/3 oz. soft cheese
2 spring onions/scallions, finely chopped
½ unwaxed lemon, zest and juice
1 tbsp finely chopped flat-leaf parsley
1 tsp nonpareille capers, drained and chopped
toast or crispbreads, to serve
salt and black pepper

PICKLED RADISHES
150 g/5½ oz. radishes, any leaves reserved
1 tbsp cider vinegar or wine vinegar
1 tsp runny honey
½ tsp salt

SERVES 2

TAKES 15 MINUTES

Slice the radishes into rounds. Mix the vinegar, honey and salt in a bowl and add the radishes. Toss and leave to macerate while you prepare the pâté.

Flake the trout into a mixing bowl and roughly run a fork through it. Add the soft cheese, spring onions, lemon zest and juice, parsley and capers and season with salt and pepper. Mix together with a fork to make a rough pâté.

Serve the pâté with toast or crispbreads, along with the pickled radishes.

CRAB, LIME & AVOCADO TOASTS

Crab on toast would easily make it onto my list of death-row meals. It is fresh, so simple and near-on perfect for a light, summer supper.

100 g/3½ oz. white crab meat
2 tbsp mayonnaise
1 spring onion/scallion, finely chopped
1 tsp nonpareille capers, drained and chopped
1 unwaxed lime
2 large slices sourdough
1 avocado, sliced
a few sprigs of dill to garnish (optional)
salt and black pepper.

SERVES 2

TAKES 15 MINUTES

In a mixing bowl, place the crab, mayonnaise, spring onion and capers. Grate in the zest of the lime then cut in in half. Squeeze in the juice from one ½, and reserve the other to serve. Season the mixture with salt and pepper and mix well together.

Toast the sourdough, then divide between plates. Arrange the sliced avocado on top, then pile on the crab. Scatter with dill, if using, and serve with the remaining ½ lime cut into wedges for squeezing over.

PRAWN COCKTAIL SALAD

Prawn cocktail is a die-hard classic that I would happily eat at least once a week. Here it is reimagined as more of a main course/entrée salad. Cayenne pepper has a kick to it, so if you don't like heat use paprika instead.

2 Little Gem/Bibb lettuces, shredded
100 g/3½ oz. cucumber, pared into ribbons
1 large avocado, thinly sliced
175 g/1⅓ cups cooked, peeled Atlantic prawns/shrimp
3 spring onions/scallions, thinly sliced
seeded crackers or crispbreads, to serve (I like Dr Karg's)

DRESSING
2 tbsp mayonnaise
1 tbsp ketchup
½ lemon, juice
½ tsp Worcestershire sauce
¼ tsp salt
pinch of cayenne pepper (or paprika), plus extra to serve
black pepper

SERVES 2

TAKES 15 MINUTES

Mix all the dressing ingredients with a good grind of black pepper

On on a platter or individual plates, pile up the lettuce. Top with the cucumber ribbons, avocado and prawns. Drizzle over the dressing and scatter with the spring onions. Dust with a little more cayenne or paprika and serve with seeded crackers or crispbreads.

TOMATO & TUNA SALAD WITH WATERCRESS PESTO

This fantastic watercress pesto will keep for 2-3 days in the fridge in a sealable container with a layer of oil on top. Toss with pasta or gnocchi or mix with crème fraîche as a dip.

600 g/1¼ lb. mixed tomatoes, sliced
220-g/8-oz. jar tuna fillets in olive oil
1 shallot, thinly sliced into rounds
crusty bread and extra pumpkin seeds, to serve

WATERCRESS PESTO
80 g/3 oz. watercress, plus extra sprigs to serve
20 g/scant ¼ cup pumpkin seeds, plus extra to serve
20 g/scant ⅓ cup finely grated Parmesan
5 tbsp extra virgin olive oil
1 small garlic clove, finely grated
½ unwaxed lemon, zest and juice
salt and black pepper

SERVES 4

TAKES 20 MINUTES

To make the pesto, place the watercress, pumpkin seeds, Parmesan, 4 tablespoons oil, garlic and lemon zest in a food processor with a pinch of salt and grind of pepper. Pulse to a coarse pesto; check the seasoning.

Tip half the pesto into a bowl and stir in the remaining 1 tablespoon olive oil and the lemon juice. The other half can be stored in the fridge (see recipe introduction).

Arrange the tomatoes over a serving plate. Drain the tuna and flake over the top. Spoon over the pesto dressing, then scatter with the shallot, extra pumpkin seeds and watercress sprigs. Serve with crusty bread.

Pictured on pages 18 and 19

CANTALOUPE & CUCUMBER SALAD WITH CHILLI & MINT

Cucumber and melon belong to the same plant family (cucurbitaceae), which may explain why they pair so harmoniously. This is a vibrant, refreshing salad that could easily be doubled to serve more.

400 g/14 oz. roughly chopped cantaloupe melon
400 g/14 oz. roughly chopped cucumber (peeled, if liked)
100 g/3½ oz. feta cheese, crumbled
2 jalapeño chillies/chiles, thinly sliced into rounds
handful mint leaves, shredded

DRESSING
2 tbsp extra virgin olive oil
1 lime, juice
1 tsp honey
salt and black pepper

SERVES 4

TAKES 15 MINUTES

Toss the melon, cucumber, feta and chillies together in a serving bowl.

Whisk the dressing ingredients with a good pinch of salt and pepper.

Pour the dressing over the salad and toss to combine. Scatter with the mint leaves to serve.

APPLE, BLUE CHEESE & LENTIL SALAD

This simple and satisfying, meal can be put together in about 15 minutes, making it the perfect fuss-free supper.

3 tbsp extra virgin olive oil, plus extra to drizzle
2 tbsp sherry vinegar (or cider vinegar or white wine vinegar)
2 tsp Dijon mustard
1 tsp runny honey
½ red onion, finely diced
500 g/3¾ cups cooked puy or green lentils
1 small apple, cut into thin matchsticks
150–200 g/5–7 oz. blue cheese (I like gorgonzola picante)
80 g/3 oz. watercress, picked into small florets
50 g/½ cup roasted, salted pecans, roughly chopped
salt and black pepper

SERVES 4

TAKES 15 MINUTES

Whisk together the oil, vinegar, mustard, honey and a good pinch of salt and pepper. Stir in the red onion and leave to sit for a couple of minutes.

Add the lentils to the bowl, stirring everything together. This can sit happily for a couple of hours.

Just before serving add the apple, cheese, watercress and pecans. Give everything a quick toss, taste and add more oil, vinegar, salt and pepper as desired. Divide between plates and serve immediately.

NO-COOK TOMATO SAUCE

Grating tomatoes is much easier than chopping them. The flesh and seeds end up creating a fresh, pulpy sauce, and the skin naturally peels away. Once mixed with a little seasoning, it is wonderful spooned over toast or tossed through cooked pasta for a fresh, light meal.

4 ripe tomatoes (about 350 g/12 oz.)
4 tbsp extra virgin olive oil
1 small garlic clove, finely grated
a squeeze of lemon juice or a dash of wine vinegar
salt and black pepper

OPTIONAL EXTRAS
basil leaves
black olives
mozzarella or burrata
anchovies
serrano ham

SERVES 3–4

TAKES 10 MINUTES

Halve the tomatoes. Press the cut side against the coarse side of a box grater. Grate over a bowl and when you reach the skin discard it.

Once all the tomatoes are grated, stir in the olive oil, garlic, a splash of lemon juice or a few drops of vinegar and season with salt and black pepper.

Spoon the sauce over toast and top with anchovies or curls of serrano ham. Or toss through cooked pasta, adding some mozzarella or burrata, basil leaves and black olives, if you like.

FIVE INGREDIENTS

SHORT SHOPPING LISTS & FABULOUS MEALS FROM JUST A HANDFUL OF INGREDIENTS.

SEA BASS WITH ROASTED FENNEL & LENTILS

Here is a sophisticated supper for two that feels so much more than the sum of its parts. Roasting has a magical effect on fennel, mellowing and sweetening its anise flavour, while also giving the lentils a nice crunch.

2 fennel bulbs
4 garlic cloves, unpeeled
400-g/14-oz. can lentils, rinsed and drained
1 lemon, juice of 1/2 and the rest in wedges
2 sea bass fillets, skin slashed in 3 places

FROM THE STORECUPBOARD
2 tbsp olive oil
3 tbsp mayonnaise (optional)
salt and black pepper

SERVES 2

TAKES 35 MINUTES

Preheat the oven to 220°C/200°C fan/425°F/Gas 7. Trim the fennel fronds and reserve. Cut each bulb lengthways into slim wedges, trimming out the hard core and discarding any gnarly outer leaves. Toss with 1 1/2 tablespoons olive oil, season with salt and spread over a roasting tray with the garlic cloves. Roast for 15 minutes.

Add the lentils to the roasting tin, squeeze over the lemon juice and stir everything together. Roast for another 10 minutes.

Meanwhile, heat a large frying pan/skillet over a high heat with the remaining 1/2 tbsp oil. Pat the sea bass fillets dry and season all over. Place skin-side down in the hot oil and cook for 3 minutes, pressing gently with a spatula to flatten them if they curl. Turn to cook on the flesh side for 30 seconds.

Divide the fennel and lentils between plates and top with a sea bass fillet. Mash the roasted garlic cloves (discarding the skin) and stir through the mayonnaise. Serve the garlicky mayo on the side, with the remaining lemon cut into wedges and the fennel fronds to garnish.

POT-ROAST CHICKEN WITH BROTHY BEANS

Cooking a roast on a weeknight? Surely no one has time for that. But pot-roasting is a brilliantly easy way to cook a whole bird, along with all its sides in the same pan and with very little washing up. Browning the chicken is the only time-consuming step, but you just need to turn it from time to time while getting on with other jobs in between. Or you can skip it if you're not bothered about eating the skin.

1.6-kg/3½-lb. whole free-range chicken
400 g/14 oz. banana shallots, peeled and halved lengthways
1 bulb of garlic, halved
about 500 g/1 lb. 2 oz. cooked cannellini beans
200 ml/¾ cup white wine

FROM THE STORECUPBOARD
1-2 tbsp olive oil
200 ml/¾ cup chicken stock
salt and black pepper

SERVES 4-5

TAKES 1 HOUR 15 MINUTES

If time allows, 30 minutes before cooking take the chicken out of the fridge and season inside and out with salt.

Heat a large lidded casserole dish (I use a 29-cm/11½-inch oval Le Creuset, approx. 5 litres/quarts in volume) over a medium heat. Pat the chicken dry with paper towel, then rub all over with 1 tablespoon olive oil. Brown in the pan, turning the bird every 3-4 minutes until the skin is as evenly golden as possible all over. Lift out and set aside on a plate.

Add the shallots and garlic to the pan with a good pinch of salt and fry for 4-5 minutes. Add a splash more oil if you need to.

Add the wine and bubble for 2-3 minutes, then add the stock and bring to a simmer. Sit the chicken back in the pan, breast-side up, and add the beans. Cover and turn the heat to low – you want just a very quiet simmer with a few tiny bubbles rising up. Cook for 50 minutes or until the chicken is completely cooked through.

Take off the heat and stand for 15 minutes before lifting the chicken out to carve. Serve in shallow bowls with the brothy beans. Crusty bread, mustardy mayonnaise and a green salad all make good accompaniments.

TIP: *Do stuff the cavity of the chicken with half a lemon and some fresh green herbs if you have them, but it's not essential.*

CARROT & PECORINO RISOTTO

The humble carrot far exceeds expectations in this wintery risotto. Its natural sweetness pairs so well with the salty tang of Pecorino, though you could also use Parmesan or Cheddar, if that's what you have to hand.

1 large onion, finely diced
300 g/10½ oz. carrots, peeled and coarsely grated
250 g/1¼ cups risotto rice (arborio or carnaroli)
125 ml/½ cup white wine
50 g/⅔ cup finely grated Pecorino Romano, plus extra to serve

FROM THE STORECUPBOARD
1 tbsp olive oil
1 tbsp unsalted butter
1 litre/quart chicken or vegetable stock
salt and black pepper

SERVES 4

TAKES 35 MINUTES

Heat the oil and butter in a large saucepan over a medium-high heat. Fry the onion with a generous pinch of salt for a couple of minutes. Add the carrots and fry, stirring regularly, for 10–12 minutes, or until the vegetables are soft and starting to caramelize.

Meanwhile heat the stock in a separate saucepan; leave over a medium-low heat to keep warm.

Stir the rice into the onion and carrots, frying for a minute or two. Then add the wine and stir until almost all the liquid has bubbled away.

One ladleful at a time, add the stock to the rice, stirring regularly. Continue until you have used most/all of the stock (about 20 minutes), the rice is 'al dente' and the risotto loose in texture. If you run out of stock before the rice is cooked, add boiling water.

Take the risotto off the heat. Stir in the Pecorino, season and cover with a lid for a couple of minutes. Serve with more grated Pecorino and a little black pepper.

TIP: *If you have some fresh herbs, like flat-leaf parsley or mint, these would work nicely, chopped and sprinkled on top.*

COURGETTE & RICOTTA TOASTS

Ricotta on toast is such a great combination. It's cool and whippy and can be accessorized with all sorts of sweet or savoury toppings. This is a fantastic summer option, when courgettes are in abundance.

3 garlic cloves, thinly sliced
500 g/17 oz. courgettes/zucchini, ends trimmed and cut into half-moons
250 g/9 oz. ricotta
1 unwaxed lemon, zest and a squeeze of juice
4 slices sourdough (seeded or rye is a good option)

FROM THE STORECUPBOARD
3 tbsp extra virgin olive oil
pinch of chilli/hot red pepper flakes (optional)
salt and black pepper

SERVES 4

TAKES 15 MINUTES

Heat the oil in a large frying pan/skillet over a medium-high heat. Fry the garlic for a minute, then add the courgettes and a good pinch of salt. Fry for about 10 minutes, stirring regularly, or until the courgettes are soft and golden.

Meanwhile, tip the ricotta into a bowl, add half the lemon zest and season with salt and pepper. Beat with a wooden spoon.

Toast the bread, then spread with the ricotta. Squeeze a little lemon juice over the courgettes, then take off the heat and pile onto the ricotta toasts. Add a pinch of chilli flakes to garnish, if you like, and the remaining lemon zest.

TOMATO, GRUYÈRE & MUSTARD TART

This makes a very nice meal on a warm evening. Serve with a crisp green salad and a glass of white wine.

320-g/$11\frac{1}{2}$-oz. sheet all-butter puff pastry
300 g/$10\frac{1}{2}$ oz. ripe tomatoes, sliced
$1\frac{1}{2}$ tbsp Dijon mustard
125 g/$1\frac{1}{4}$ cups coarsely grated Gruyère
8 cornichons (about 40 g/$1\frac{1}{2}$ oz.), chopped or sliced

FROM THE STORECUPBOARD
$\frac{1}{2}$ tsp dried thyme or mixed herbs
salt and black pepper

SERVES 4

TAKES 45 MINUTES

Preheat the oven to 200°C/180°C fan/400°F/Gas 6. Unroll the pastry on its paper and place on a large baking sheet. Score a 2-cm/1-inch border around the edge of the pastry (taking care not to cut all the way through), then prick the base all over with a fork. Bake for 15 minutes.

Meanwhile, cut the tomatoes into 5-mm/$\frac{1}{4}$-inch slices. Lay out on a couple of layers of paper towel to soak up the extra liquid and sprinkle with a little salt.

Take the pastry out of the oven. Spread the base with the mustard, then sprinkle evenly with the Gruyère. Arrange the tomato slices over the top, season with salt and pepper and scatter with the dried herbs. Return the tart to the oven for about 20 minutes until puffed up and golden. Cool for 5–10 minutes before scattering with the cornichons. Slice and serve warm or at room temperature with a crisp green salad, if you like.

Pictured on pages 34–35

SAUSAGE & CAVOLO NERO PASTA

Why are sausages so often sold in packs of six? It's rarely enough for four people, but a bit too much for two. Well, if you squeeze the sausagemeat from it's skins, fry and toss with pasta, leafy greens and cream, you end up with a generous, one-pan meal for four.

200 g/7 oz. cavolo nero
1 onion, finely diced
6 free-range pork sausages
400 g/14 oz. penne
150 ml/²/₃ cup single/light cream

FROM THE STORECUPBOARD
2 tbsp olive oil
grated Parmesan, to serve (optional)
salt and black pepper

SERVES 4

TAKES 15 MINUTES

Strip the cavolo nero leaves from the stalks. Roughly shred the leaves and set aside. Thinly slice the tender parts of the stalks and discard the tougher ends.

Heat the oil in a large sauté pan or shallow casserole over a medium-high heat. Add the onion and thinly sliced cavolo nero stalks with a pinch of salt and fry for 3–4 minutes.

Meanwhile bring a large saucepan of salted water to a rolling boil. Add the pasta and cook for 1 minute less than the pack instructions.

Squeeze the sausages from their skins into the pan with the onions, break up with a wooden spoon and fry for 3–4 minutes. Add the cavolo nero leaves and fry for another 4–5 minutes until the leaves have wilted and the sausagemeat is cooked through.

Scoop out a mugful of the cooking water, then drain the pasta. Tip the drained pasta into the pan with the sausages and cavolo nero. Add the cream, a glug of the cooking water (and a squeeze of lemon juice if you have it) and toss over the heat for a minute until everything is coated in a glossy, creamy sauce. Season with salt and pepper and serve with grated Parmesan, if you like.

SMOKY BACON, CORN & WHITE BEAN CHOWDER

This soup has split pea and ham vibes: smoky, earthy and soothing. Not only do cannellini beans provide a boost of protein, they also blend to a lovely, velvety texture.

150 g/5½ oz. smoked bacon lardons
2 large leeks, cleaned, halved lengthways and sliced
150 g/5½ oz. frozen sweetcorn
240 g/8½ oz. cooked cannellini beans
250 ml/1 cup whole milk

FROM THE STORECUPBOARD
500 ml/2 cups chicken or vegetable stock
squeeze of lemon juice (optional)
salt and black pepper

SERVES 4

TAKES 30 MINUTES

Place the lardons in a large saucepan over a medium heat. Cook them, stirring regularly, for about 10 minutes until crisped up and all their fat has released. Scoop out of the pan with a slotted spoon (leaving the fat in there) and set aside on a plate lined with kitchen towel.

Add the leeks to the pan with a pinch of salt and sweat in the bacon fat for 8–10 minutes until soft. Add the sweetcorn, beans and stock. Simmer for 5 minutes.

Blend half of the soup with the milk, plus a grind of black pepper (and a splash of lemon juice if you have it) until smooth. Return to the pan and mix together. Check the seasoning and add more salt as desired. Reheat and serve topped with the crispy lardons.

MARMALADE CHICKEN WITH BUTTERY MASH

Sticky, bitter and citrussy marmalade definitely has scope beyond toast. It makes a brilliant marinade for traybaked chicken. I like to make my mash by baking whole potatoes and scooping out the insides. It takes a bit longer (though you have the oven on for the chicken here anyway), but it means you end up with the skins, which can be saved and then re-baked for another meal.

4 baking potatoes
150 g/5½ oz. Seville orange marmalade
3 tbsp soy sauce
2 tbsp Dijon mustard
1 kg/2¼ lbs. chicken drumsticks

FROM THE STORECUPBOARD
large knob/pat of butter
splash of milk
salt and black pepper

SERVES 4

TAKES 1 HOUR

Preheat the oven to 200°C/180°C fan/400°F/Gas 6. Pierce the potatoes all over with a fork, place on a baking sheet and bake for 15 minutes.

Meanwhile, whisk together the marmalade, soy and mustard. Place the chicken in a baking dish and pour over the marinade, turning the pieces to make sure they're coated. Season with a little black pepper.

Add the chicken to the oven and roast alongside the potatoes for 45 minutes. Baste the chicken in the marinade every 15 minutes or so. If at any point the sauce looks like it's starting to darken too much, stir it up and add a splash of water.

Let the chicken stand for 5 minutes, while you carefully split open the potatoes (use clean oven gloves to handle them as they'll be hot) and tip the flesh into a mixing bowl with a knob/pat of butter and a splash of milk. Season and mash until smooth, then serve with the chicken and sticky juices, plus some steamed green vegetables too, if you like.

BAKED BROCCOLI & CHEDDAR FRITTATA

Frittata is the archetypal midweek meal, perfect for using up what's in the fridge. I especially like this oven-baked method because, even though I am a trained cook, I still haven't mastered a frittata perfectly cooked on the hob/stovetop. The base often browns too much and then there's the conundrum of how to cook the middle – do I risk flipping it or put it under the grill/broiler? This recipe removes all that jeopardy.

200 g/7 oz. Tenderstem broccoli, thicker stems halved lengthways
6 large eggs
75 ml/1/3 cup whole milk
100 g/1 cup grated mature/ sharp Cheddar
3 spring onions/scallions, finely chopped

FROM THE STORECUPBOARD
1 tbsp olive oil
salt and black pepper

SERVES 2–3

TAKES 30 MINUTES

Preheat the oven to 180°C/160°C fan/375°F/Gas 4. Toss the broccoli with the oil and a pinch of salt and spread over a baking tray. Roast for 10 minutes.

Meanwhile, line a small-medium baking tin/pan (approx. 16 x 26 cm/6¼ x 10¼ inches) with baking parchment, making sure it's a single piece that covers the base and sides (so the egg mixture can't seep out).

In a mixing bowl, whisk the eggs, milk and ½ teaspoon salt together with a grind of black pepper. Stir in about three-quarters of the Cheddar and all of the spring onions. Tip into the lined baking tin.

Arrange the roasted broccoli over the top, pressing it lightly into the egg mixture. Scatter evenly with the remaining Cheddar and give it another grind of black pepper.

Bake for 18–20 minutes, or until just set. Serve in squares with salad, or in ciabatta rolls with sliced avocado and a hot sauce of your choice.

JUST ONE PAN

SIMPLE RECIPES THAT OFFER MAXIMUM FLAVOUR & MINIMUM CLEAR UP.

FRAGRANT COCONUT NOODLE SOUP

I could eat this, without fail, at least once a week. Quite often I'll infuse the broth in advance and then simply reheat it with prawns and vegetables to serve. I find that curry pastes vary wildly in heat levels, so I'd always suggest starting small if it's a paste you've not used before. Also, a good tip on makrut lime leaves: you can buy them fresh (which are much more fragrant than dried) in lots of major supermarkets and they freeze very well. So buy a bag, then stash any extra in the freezer for next time.

1 tbsp vegetable oil, plus extra to toss
1 onion or shallot, roughly chopped
1 garlic clove, bashed
2–3 tbsp Thai red curry paste (depending on how spicy it is)
500 ml/2 cups chicken or vegetable stock
4 fresh makrut lime leaves, roughly torn
180 g/6½ oz. dried flat rice noodles
1 tbsp fish sauce
1 tsp sugar or maple syrup
1 lime, juice
400-ml/14-oz. can coconut milk
150 g/5½ oz. baby chestnut mushrooms, quartered
160 g/1 generous cup raw king prawns/jumbo shrimp
Thai basil leaves, to garnish

SERVES 2–3

TAKES 35 MINUTES

Heat the oil in a large saucepan over a medium-high heat. Fry the onion and garlic for a minute, then add the curry paste and fry for 2 minutes more, stirring regularly. Add the stock and lime leaves. Simmer gently for 20 minutes to infuse.

Meanwhile prepare the noodles according to the pack instructions, straining them once they're tender (taste to check) and running under cold water to stop the cooking. Toss with a little oil to prevent sticking and divide between serving bowls.

Strain or scoop out the aromatics from the broth and discard. Stir in the fish sauce, the sugar (or maple syrup) and juice of half a lime, then the coconut milk. Taste, adjusting the balance of fish sauce and lime juice as needed.

Add the mushrooms to the pan and simmer for 5 minutes, then add the prawns and simmer for another 3–4 minutes until cooked through. Ladle the soup over the rice noodles and garnish with the Thai basil leaves to serve.

SAUSAGES WITH MUSTARDY LEEKS & SWEET POTATOES

Unless the skins of the sweet potatoes are particularly gnarly, it's not worth peeling them. The skin holds lots of fibre and adds a nice textural contrast in this rich and comforting gratin.

1½ tbsp olive oil
2 leeks, halved lengthways and thinly sliced
1 tsp salt
600 g/1¼ lb. sweet potatoes
200 ml/¾ cup whole milk
150 ml/⅔ cup double/heavy cream
3 tbsp Dijon mustard
8 good-quality pork and herb sausages
black pepper

SERVES 4

TAKES 1 HOUR

Preheat the oven to 200°C/180°C fan/400°F/Gas 6.

Heat the oil in a large, ovenproof frying pan/skillet or shallow casserole/Dutch oven over a medium heat. Fry the leeks with the salt for 7–8 minutes until sweet and soft.

Meanwhile prepare the sweet potatoes. Give the skins a wash, then slice as thinly as you can into rounds.

Whisk together the milk, cream and mustard with a good grind of black pepper. Add to the pan, then tip in the potatoes. Mix everything together, then cover with a lid and cook gently for 5 minutes.

Remove the lid. Arrange the sausages on top of the potatoes and transfer the pan to the oven and cook for 25–30 minutes, turning the sausages halfway through the cooking time. Let stand for 5 minutes before serving with green vegetables, if liked.

HARISSA CHICKEN, ARTICHOKES & GIANT COUSCOUS

Here the giant couscous acts a bit like paella rice, soaking up all the wonderful flavours of the chicken and the harissa as it swells. I think one large chicken thigh will suffice if serving this with a green vegetable or salad, though you may prefer two chicken thighs per person for hungrier mouths.

4 large skin-on, bone-in chicken thighs (about 175 g/6 oz. each)
1 onion, finely diced
2 garlic cloves, finely chopped
100 g/3½ oz. tomatoes, finely diced
2 tbsp rose harissa (I like Belazu)
250 g/1½ cups giant couscous, rinsed
350 ml/1½ cups chicken stock
280-g/10-oz. jar artichokes in oil
salt and black pepper
natural/plain yogurt and lemon wedges, to serve

SERVES 4

TAKES 1 HOUR

Preheat the oven to 200°C/180°C fan/400°F/Gas 6. Season the chicken all over and place skin-side down in a large ovenproof sauté pan or shallow casserole/Dutch oven. Turn the heat to medium-high heat and fry the chicken for 7–8 minutes until the skin is browned (there's no need to add any oil as the chicken skin will release fat as it cooks). Turn and cook the flesh side for 2 minutes, then lift out of the pan and set aside.

There should be enough rendered fat from the chicken left in the pan to fry the onions and garlic, if not add a splash from the jar of artichokes. Fry the onion and garlic with a big pinch of salt for 5-6 minutes until starting to soften, then add the tomatoes and fry for 2 minutes more.

Add the harissa and fry, stirring, for 2 minutes then stir in the rinsed couscous and fry for a minute to coat it in the harissa. Tip the stock into the pan, then return the chicken skin-side up. Drain the artichokes and scatter around the chicken.

Grind a little black pepper over everything, then transfer the pan to the oven. Bake for 30–35 minutes until the chicken is golden and cooked through, and all the stock is absorbed. Stand for 5-10 minutes before serving with lemon wedges and a little yogurt, if liked.

COD WITH LEMONY POTATOES, TOMATOES & OLIVES

Slow-roasted potatoes in garlic, lemon juice and stock are pretty hard to beat. Aside from a bit of prep at the start, this dish practically takes care of itself. You could easily double up the quantities to serve 4 people.

350 g/¾ lb. waxy potatoes (such as Charlotte or new potatoes)
2½ tbsp extra virgin olive oil
150 g/5½ oz. tomatoes, sliced
50 g/½ cup stoned/pitted kalamata olives, halved
2 garlic cloves, sliced
¾ tsp salt
100 ml/scant ½ cup chicken stock
1 lemon, juice of ½ and the rest sliced
2 x 120-g/4½-oz. skinless cod fillets
salt and black pepper

SERVES 2

TAKES 1 HOUR

Preheat the oven to 200°C/180°C fan/400°F/Gas 6.

Slice the potatoes as thinly as possible, then toss in a large mixing bowl with 2 tablespoons oil, the tomatoes, olives, garlic, salt and a grind of pepper. Arrange in a medium baking dish (about 1 litre/1 quart in volume), then pour over the stock and squeeze over the lemon juice.

Bake for 20 minutes, then stir the vegetables carefully, spooning some of the liquid from the base over the top. Bake for another 20 minutes.

At this point take the cod out of the fridge, remove from the packaging, pat dry with paper towels and season with salt and pepper.

Sit the cod fillets on top of the potatoes and drizzle over the remaining ½ tablespoon oil. Arrange the sliced lemon over the top and bake for a final 10 minutes. Serve with a green salad, if you like.

TAMARIND FISH CURRY

Tamarind is not an ingredient I cook with very often. It's a tropical fruit and the pulp, which is widely available to buy in jars, is sweet and sour and gives a lovely tang to this uncomplicated fish curry. Tamarind pastes vary in sourness, so it's best to start by adding a little and build up. You can also make the sauce in advance and reheat before adding the fish.

1 tbsp vegetable or sunflower oil
1 onion, finely chopped
2 garlic cloves, finely chopped
15 g/½ oz. fresh root ginger, peeled and finely chopped
8 curry leaves
½ tsp salt
2 tsp garam masala
1 tsp black mustard seeds
400-g/14-oz. can chopped tomatoes
2 x 120-g/4½-oz. firm white fish fillets (such as cod, hake or haddock)
1-2 tbsp tamarind paste
½ tsp sugar
steamed basmati rice, to serve
coriander/cilantro leaves, to garnish

SERVES 2

TAKES 25 MINUTES

Heat the oil over a medium-high heat in a large frying pan or shallow casserole/Dutch oven for which you have a lid. Fry the onion, garlic, ginger, curry leaves and salt for 8 minutes until turning golden. Stir in the garam masala and mustard seeds and fry for 2 minutes more.

Add the chopped tomatoes, then fill the empty can with 150 ml/⅔ cup water and add to the pan. Simmer gently for 7–8 minutes. Meanwhile, season the fish with a little salt and set aside.

Stir 1 tablespoon tamarind paste and the sugar into the tomato sauce and bring to a simmer. Taste and add more tamarind as desired.

Nestle the fish into the sauce, cover with a lid, and lower the heat to a gentle simmer. Cook for 7–9 minutes until the fish is cooked through. Serve with basmati rice and coriander leaves to garnish.

ONE-PAN BEEF, LENTIL & RICOTTA 'LASAGNE'

I love lasagne as much as the next person, but it doesn't really fit into the 'weeknight' category. So here's a little short-cut version that requires one pan and can be ready in about 45 minutes.

1 tbsp olive oil
1 onion, finely diced
1 large carrot, finely diced
1 celery stalk/rib, finely diced
½ tsp salt, plus more to taste
500 g/1 lb. 2 oz. British beef mince/ground beef (I use 12% fat)
1 tbsp tomato purée/paste
400-g/14-oz. can green lentils in water, drained and rinsed
400-g/14-oz. can chopped tomatoes
3 tbsp whole milk
40 g/scant ⅔ cup finely grated Parmesan
250-g/9-oz. tub ricotta
5 fresh lasagne sheets (about 125 g/4½ oz.), halved lengthways
black pepper
green salad, to serve (optional)

SERVES 4

TAKES 45 MINUTES

Heat the oil over a medium-high heat in a large ovenproof sauté pan or shallow casserole/Dutch oven. Fry the onion, carrot and celery with ½ teaspoon salt for 5 minutes.

Push the vegetables to one side of the pan. Add the meat to the other side with a good pinch of salt. Leave for 1 minute, then break up with a wooden spoon and fry with the vegetables for 5–6 minutes.

Stir in the tomato purée and cook for a minute, then add the lentils and tomatoes. Half-fill the tomato can with water and add also to the pan. Season with black pepper and simmer gently for 20 minutes. Add the milk and cook for a final 5 minutes. (The sauce can be made up to this stage in advance and reheated to continue the recipe.)

Meanwhile, mix half of the Parmesan into the ricotta and season lightly.

Preheat the grill/broiler to high. Nestle the lasagne sheets into the sauce (use a fork and a spoon to help manoeuvre the sauce around and over them). Simmer for 2–3 minutes.

Spoon the ricotta in dollops over the top, scatter over the remaining Parmesan and pop under the grill (on a shelf about two-thirds of the way up the oven) for 5 minutes until bubbling and golden. Serve with a green salad, if you like.

TIP: *Speed things up further by using 250 g/9 oz. ready chopped 'soffritto' (onion, carrot and celery).*

CHICKEN, MINT & FETA MEATBALLS

Minced/ground chicken is such an underrated ingredient. It is by far my top choice for making meatballs with light, summery flavours. These meatballs can be paired with any carb you like.

500 g/1 lb. 2 oz. minced/ ground chicken
1 courgette/zucchini, trimmed and coarsely grated
small handful mint leaves, shredded
3/4 tsp salt, plus more to taste
1/2 tsp ground cinnamon
1/2 tsp ground allspice
1/2 unwaxed lemon, zest
200 g/7 oz. feta, crumbled
1 tbsp olive oil
3 garlic cloves, unpeeled and bashed
400-g/14-oz. can finely chopped tomatoes
1 tsp honey
black pepper
pasta, couscous, rice or garlic bread, to serve

SERVES 4

TAKES 45 MINUTES

Preheat the oven to 200°C/180°C fan/400°F/Gas 6.

In a large mixing bowl, place the minced chicken, courgette, mint, salt and spices, lemon zest and a good grind of black pepper. Mix together with your hands until combined. Gently combine half the crumbled feta into the mixture. Roll into 12 large meatballs.

Heat the oil in a large ovenproof frying pan/skiller or sauté pan over a medium-high heat. Add the meatballs and the garlic cloves. Cook for 7–8 minutes, turning the meatballs regularly to brown.

Tip the canned tomatoes into the pan, then fill the can with 100 ml/scant 1/2 cup water and also add to the pan. Add the honey, a pinch of salt and a grind of pepper, shaking everything to combine. Transfer to the oven and cook for 10 minutes.

Scatter the remaining feta over the top of the meatballs and sauce, and roast for a final 10 minutes. Serve with couscous, pasta, rice or garlic bread.

ADOBO-STYLE CHICKEN & CAULIFLOWER

Adobo is a Filipino dish which involves braising in vinegar and soy. The resulting flavours are deeply savoury, tangy and quite uniquely delicious – I urge you to try it if you have not already. This is definitely a dish you can prepare in advance and reheat for weeknight guests.

5 tbsp cider vinegar
5 tbsp light soy sauce
2 garlic cloves, 1 crushed and 1 thinly sliced
10 black peppercorns
1 bay leaf
4 large skin-on, bone-in chicken thighs (about 175 g/6 oz. each)
1 tbsp olive oil
1 large onion, halved and thinly sliced
400-g/14-oz. cauliflower (1 small), cut into large florets
1 tbsp soft light brown sugar

TO SERVE
sliced red chilli/chile (optional)
steamed rice

SERVES 4

TAKES 1 HOUR, plus marinating

In a marinade bag or non-metallic mixing bowl place the vinegar, soy, crushed garlic clove, peppercorns and bay leaf. Add the chicken and let marinate for 20 minutes or up to 2 hours.

Preheat the oven to 180°C/160°C fan/350°F/Gas 4.

Heat the oil in a large sauté pan or shallow casserole/Dutch coven over a high heat. Lift the chicken from the marinade (reserve the marinade), pat the skin dry and fry skin-side down for 9 minutes until golden, then turn and fry the flesh side for 1–2 minutes. Lift out of the pan and set aside.

Add the onion, sliced garlic clove and cauliflower to the pan and fry for 5 minutes until starting to turn golden. Tip in the reserved marinade, sugar and 150 ml/scant ½ cup water and bring to a simmer for 3–4 minutes.

Nestle the chicken back into the pan, transfer to the oven and cook for 30 minutes. Stand for 5 minutes before sprinkling with sliced chillies, if using, and serving with steamed rice.

READY IN 20

FUSS-FREE MEALS
WITH FAST FLAVOURS
& SMART SHORTCUTS.

SPAGHETTI WITH PRAWNS & CARAMELIZED FENNEL

I love a pasta sauce that comes together in the time it takes for the spaghetti to boil. Here, it's just enough time for the fennel to turn nutty and sweet.

1 fennel bulb, fronds trimmed and reserved
2–3 tbsp extra virgin olive oil
1 shallot, finely diced
2 garlic cloves, finely diced
½ tsp salt, plus more for the pasta water and prawns/shrimp
180 g/6 oz. dried spaghetti
pinch of chilli/hot red pepper flakes
165 g/1 generous cup raw king prawns/jumbo shrimp
½ unwaxed lemon, zest and juice
black pepper

SERVES 2

TAKES 15 MINUTES

Start by preparing the fennel. Halve it lengthways, cut out the thick core, then slice it widthways as thinly as you can.

Heat 2 tablespoons oil in a large frying pan/skillet over a medium-high heat. Fry the fennel, shallot, garlic and ½ teaspoon salt for about 10 minutes until soft and starting to caramelize.

Once the vegetables are frying, fill a saucepan with boiling salted water and cook the spaghetti for 1 minute less than the pack instructions. Scoop out a mugful of the cooking water before draining.

Stir the chilli flakes into the fennel, then push everything to one side of the pan. Add a splash more oil to the empty side of the pan and let it heat for a minute. Season the prawns lightly, then add to the hot oil. Leave for a minute to cook, then turn and cook on the other side for a minute, then stir everything together.

Tip the drained pasta into the frying pan. Add a glug of the cooking water, the lemon zest and juice and a grind of black pepper. Toss everything over the heat for a minute, then divide between plates, garnish with the fennel fronds and serve.

EGG ON TOAST, MUMBAI-STYLE

If either eggs or cheese on toast are a regular fallback supper for you, then this quick and tasty hybrid will likely float your boat. Known as eggs kejriwal, the dish originated in the cafés of south Mumbai and gained popularity in the UK thanks to Dishoom's brunch menu. Use mango chutney if you prefer a sweeter note, or tomato chutney for a more savoury tang.

75 g/¾ cup coarsely grated mature/Sharp Cheddar
2 tbsp finely chopped red onion
1 mild green chilli/chile, thinly sliced
handful coriander/cilantro leaves, roughly chopped
2 slices sourdough bread
salted butter, for spreading
1–2 tbsp mango (or tomato) chutney
½ tbsp olive oil
2 large eggs
salt and black pepper

SERVES 2

TAKES 20 MINUTES

Preheat the oven to 200°C/180°C fan/400°F/Gas 6. Mix the Cheddar, onion, most of the chilli and most of the coriander together in a bowl.

Lightly toast the sourdough and spread with a little butter, then place on a foil-lined baking tray. Spread each with chutney, then arrange the cheese mixture on top, making sure to cover it right to the edges. Bake for 4–5 minutes, or until the cheese has melted.

Meanwhile, heat the oil in a frying pan over a medium-high heat. Fry the eggs until the whites are set, basting the yolks with a little oil to help them firm up on top.

Divide the toasts between plates and top each with an egg. Season with salt and pepper and scatter with the remaining coriander and chilli.

REUBEN-STYLE SMOKED TURKEY BAGELS

This is a playful twist on the classic North American Reuben sandwich. It has the tangy dressing, piles of punchy sauerkraut, nutty Swiss cheese, but goes a little off piste with smoked turkey and a bagel base. It makes a winning, filling meal, when you're short of time.

2 bagels, halved
salted butter, for spreading
120 g/1¼ cups coarsely grated Gruyère cheese
150 g/5½ oz. sliced roast or smoked turkey
200 g/7 oz. sauerkraut (I like Vadasz)
extra pickles, to serve (optional)

DRESSING
2 tbsp tomato ketchup
2 tbsp mayonnaise
2 tbsp hot horseradish
squeeze of lemon juice
salt and black pepper

SERVES 2

TAKES 15 MINUTES

Preheat the grill/broiler to high. Mix the all the dressing ingredients together and season with salt and pepper.

Toast the bagels lightly, then butter lightly. Arrange on a baking tray and spread a little of the dressing on each half, then pile on the cheese. Pop under the grill for 1–2 minutes or until melted.

Top the bagels with smoked turkey and pile on the sauerkraut. Drizzle over a little more dressing and serve with extra pickles on the side, if liked.

SESAME TUNA SOBA NOODLES

This is an all-time favourite in my house, the kind of meal I make on a Friday night instead of a takeaway. Aside from chopping a bit of veg there's very little preparation involved. Mirin is a type of sweet rice wine (with a low alcohol content) which is used in marinades and dressings. You could use rice vinegar instead, and add more maple syrup to taste.

100 g/3½ oz. frozen edamame
100 g/3½ oz. broccoli, in small florets or chunks of stalk
200 g/7 oz. fresh or 125 g/4½ oz. dried soba noodles (I like Itsu's fresh Restaurant Ramen Soba)
1 small, ripe avocado, chopped
3 spring onions/scallions, finely chopped

MIRIN DRESSING
3 tbsp soy sauce
2 tbsp mirin
1 tsp maple syrup
1 tsp toasted sesame oil, plus a splash more for the noodles
½ tsp finely grated fresh root ginger

SESAME TUNA
1 tbsp vegetable or sunflower oil
2 tbsp sesame seeds (ideally a mix of black and white)
2 x 120-g/4½-oz. fresh tuna steaks
salt and black pepper

SERVES 2

TAKES 20 MINUTES

Bring a large saucepan of water to the boil. Add the edamame and cook until they start rising to the top. Add the broccoli and simmer for another 2 minutes. Scoop the vegetables out with a slotted spoon and set aside on paper towels.

Add the noodles to the boiling water and cooking according to pack instructions. Drain in a sieve/strainer, rinse under the cold tap, then shake dry. Toss with a splash of sesame oil and divide between two shallow serving bowls. Top with the edamame, broccoli, avocado and spring onions.

Meanwhile mix the mirin dressing ingredients together. Spoon a little over the noodles and vegetables.

For the sesame tuna, heat the vegetable oil in a medium frying pan/skillet over a medium-high heat. Place the sesame seeds on a plate. Season the tuna steaks with salt and pepper, then press into the sesame seeds, coating all over. Fry in the hot oil for 1–2 minutes on each side, depending on the thickness of the steaks and how well you like them cooked.

Slice the tuna steaks and arrange on top of the noodles and vegetables. Spoon over a little more mirin dressing and serve immediately.

SALMON & COUSCOUS TRAYBAKE WITH TZATZIKI

This is a pretty standard weeknight supper in my house. There are a few different elements and it requires a bit of coordination, but everything comes together quite quickly to make a satisfying meal. I find that most supermarket salmon fillets haven't had the scales removed from the skin, so I tend to take it off before roasting. I also highly recommend wholewheat couscous, it's nuttier and more textured.

1 red onion, cut into thin wedges
1 Romano red pepper, deseeded and cut into wedges
2 tbsp olive oil
150 g/5½ oz. wholewheat couscous
2 x 120-g/4½-oz. salmon fillets
1 small lemon, halved
1 tsp smoked paprika
salt and black pepper

TZATZIKI
200 g/7 oz. cucumber
¼ tsp salt
150 g/scant ¾ cup Greek-style yogurt
1 small garlic clove, finely grated
8 mint leaves, shredded

SERVES 2

TAKES 20 MINUTES

Preheat the oven to 220°C/200°C fan/425°F/Gas 7.

Toss the onion and red pepper with 1 tablespoon oil and spread over a baking tray. Season and roast for 10 minutes.

Meanwhile place the couscous in a mixing bowl with a small pinch of salt. Pour over 250 ml/1 cup just-boiled water. Cover the bowl with a plate and set aside for 5 minutes.

For the tzatziki, use a box grater to coarsely grate the cucumber into a sieve/strainer. Mix with ¼ teaspoon salt and set over a bowl to catch the excess water.

After 10 minutes, take the vegetables out of the oven, give them a stir and push to one side of the tray. Fork the couscous, then tip into the tray and spread out. Spoon the vegetables on top. Add the salmon fillets to the tray. Drizzle the remaining 1 tablespoon oil over everything, squeeze over the lemon halves and add the shells to the tray. Sprinkle over the paprika and season everything with salt and pepper. Return the tray to the oven for 8 minutes.

Finish the tzatziki by pressing the cucumber with the back of a spoon to extract as much liquid as possible (discard the liquid), then tip into a bowl and mix with the yogurt, garlic and mint. Serve alongside the salmon.

CREAMY TOMATO & PANCETTA GNOCCHI

Gnocchi is such a handy ingredient to have on stand-by. The fresh packs from the supermarket will happily sit in the fridge for a few weeks, and when you need a quick meal, it cooks in under 3 minutes. This is a speedy weeknight supper that everybody loves.

1 tbsp olive oil
1 shallot, finely diced (or 1 tbsp finely chopped onion)
80 g/3 oz. diced smoked pancetta
200 g/7 oz. fresh, ripe tomatoes, finely chopped (or a 200-g/7-oz. can chopped tomatoes)
250 g/9 oz. fresh gnocchi
3 tbsp single/light cream
salt and black pepper
grated Parmesan, to serve
basil leaves, to garnish (optional)

SERVES 2

TAKES 15 MINUTES

Heat the oil in a large frying pan/skillet over a medium heat. Fry the shallot and pancetta together for 6–7 minutes until the pancetta is turning golden.

Tip the tomatoes into the pan and cook for 4–5 minutes, stirring regularly, until the tomatoes have softened and broken down.

Bring a large saucepan of water to the boil and cook the gnocchi according to pack instructions. As soon as they float to the top of the water, scoop out with a slotted spoon (or drain in a sieve/strainer if easier) and transfer to the frying pan. Add the cream and toss everything over the heat for 30 seconds.

Check the seasoning, adding salt and pepper as needed, and serve with grated Parmesan. Some basil leaves to garnish would be nice, too, if you have them.

CHICKPEA, FETA & CORIANDER SALAD

Here is a quick throw-together salad that has heaps of flavour. For a meat-free alternative, swap the bacon for chopped sun-dried tomatoes.

4 rashers/slices streaky bacon
240 g/8½ oz. cooked queen chickpeas from a jar, drained
75 g/3 oz. feta, crumbled
100 g/3½ oz. cucumber, diced
15 g/½ oz. coriander/cilantro, roughly chopped
1 tbsp extra virgin olive oil
1 lime, juice
½ tsp honey
salt and black pepper

SERVES 2

TAKES 15 MINUTES

Lay the bacon rashers in a large non-stick frying pan/skillet and set over a medium-high heat. Fry for 4–5 minutes on each side, or until golden and crisp. Set aside on paper towel to soak up the excess fat.

Meanwhile, place the chickpeas, feta, cucumber and coriander in a large mixing bowl.

In a separate bowl, whisk the oil, lime juice, and honey with a little salt and pepper.

Chop the bacon and add to the bowl, then pour over the dressing. Toss together and serve.

COBB SALAD

This legendary American salad is known for its colourful rows of toppings and satisfying ingredients like crispy bacon, avocado and blue cheese. The original often includes chopped turkey, which would be a welcome addition here too.

8 rashers/slices streaky/fatty bacon
2 heads romaine lettuce, chopped
4 hard-boiled eggs, chopped
4 tomatoes, chopped
1 avocado, chopped
1 yellow or orange (bell) pepper, deseeded and chopped

BLUE CHEESE DRESSING
6 tbsp whole milk
6 tbsp soured cream
1½ tbsp cider vinegar
1½ tsp honey
150 g/5½ oz. blue cheese (such as Stilton or St Agur), crumbled
salt and black pepper

SERVES 4

TAKES 20 MINUTES

Place the bacon in a large frying pan/skillet and cook for about 4–5 minutes on each side, or until crisp and golden. Set aside on paper towels to soak up the excess fat.

Meanwhile, whisk together the milk, soured cream, vinegar and honey. Add the blue cheese, and stir together. Season to taste.

Place the chopped lettuce in the base of a serving bowl. Spoon over about half of the dressing. Roughly chop the bacon and arrange, along with the other ingredients, in lines over the top of the lettuce. Serve with the remaining dressing on the side.

Pictured on pages 78–79

STEAK & ASPARAGUS RICE BOWLS WITH MISO-MUSTARD SAUCE

Salty from miso and with a hit of nose-tingling fieriness from English mustard, this is one of the best sauces to serve with a steak. If you make the sauce in advance (it'll keep in the fridge for 2–3 days), then the rest of the meal can be knocked up in about 10 minutes.

2 x 200-g/7-oz. rib-eye steaks
2 tsp sunflower oil
200 g/7 oz. asparagus, ends trimmed
250-g/9-oz. pouch of cooked rice (basmati or jasmine)
salt and black pepper
black sesame seeds (or white ones, toasted), to serve

MISO-MUSTARD SAUCE
3 tbsp single/light cream
2 tbsp white miso paste
1 tbsp soy sauce
2 tsp English mustard
1½ tsp runny honey
1 small garlic clove, chopped
squeeze of lemon juice

SERVES 2

TAKES 20 MINUTES

If you can, take the steaks out of the fridge 30 minutes before you plan to cook them. Season with salt and pepper.

Place all the sauce ingredients and 1–2 tablespoons water in a small, high-powered blender and whizz until smooth; set aside.

Set a frying pan/skillet or griddle pan over a high heat (or use a hot barbecue). Pat the steaks dry and brush all over with 1 teaspoon oil. Cook for 2–3 minutes on each side for medium-rare; set aside to rest for 5 minutes.

Wipe out the pan. Toss the asparagus with the remaining oil, and season lightly with salt. Toss into the pan and fry for about 2 minutes until charred in places.

Meanwhile heat the rice according to the pack instructions and divide between serving plates. Halve the asparagus and pile on top. Then slice the steak and arrange on the plates. Spoon over any resting juices, then drizzle over the dressing (you may not need it all). Scatter with sesame seeds and serve.

EVERYDAY PROTEIN

SATISFYING PLATES, DESIGNED TO NOURISH, REFUEL & ENERGIZE.

SALMON & CHICKPEA 'CAESAR'

This isn't quite a traditional Caesar salad, but the Parmesan dressing provides a familiar flavour and the chickpeas add the crunch in place of the croûtons.

1 unwaxed lemon, zest and ½ tbsp juice
1 garlic clove, finely grated or crushed
1 tbsp olive oil
2 x 120-g/4½-oz. salmon fillets, skin-on
160 g/6 oz. cooked queen chickpeas from a jar, drained
2 tbsp natural/plain yogurt
2 tbsp mayonnaise
¼ tsp Worcestershire sauce
20 g/scant ⅓ cup finely grated Parmesan, plus extra to serve
1 head romaine lettuce, roughly chopped
salt and black pepper

SERVES 2

TAKES 20 MINUTES

Preheat the grill/broiler to high; place a rack on the top shelf. Grate the lemon zest into a bowl. Add half of the grated garlic, the oil and a good pinch of salt and pepper.

Brush the salmon fillets all over with about half of this oil mixture. Place on a foil-lined tray and grill for 7–8 minutes. (If you like the skin crispy, grill for about 6 minutes on the skin, then turn and finish the flesh for 2 minutes, or just cook flesh-side up for the entire time if you aren't eating the skin.)

Meanwhile, place a frying pan/skillet over a medium-high heat. Toss the chickpeas in the remaining oil mixture, then add to the pan. Fry, tossing regularly, until golden and crisp, about 10 minutes.

Meanwhile, mix together the remaining grated garlic, yogurt, mayonnaise, Worcestershire sauce, lemon juice and Parmesan and season with salt and pepper. You may need to loosen it with a tiny splash of water if it's too thick.

Divide the lettuce between serving plates. Top with the chickpeas, then add the flaked salmon and spoon over the dressing. Scatter with a little more Parmesan, if you like.

TIP: *If you have a dual-zone air fryer, it's great for cooking both the chickpeas and salmon at the same time. (Salmon at 180°C/350°F and chickpeas at 200°C/400°F for 10–15 minutes.)*

VIETNAMESE-STYLE MONKFISH NOODLES WITH GREEN BEANS & DILL

This is a sensational dish that requires a little effort, but is wholly worth it. I think it's perfect for a dinner for two if you're looking to impress. You will be amazed at how well the dill marries all the flavours together.

about 200 g/7 oz. monkfish, cut into 3-cm/1¼-in. chunks
2 tbsp vegetable or sunflower oil
1 large onion, halved and finely sliced
100 g/3½ oz. fine green beans, trimmed and halved
1 large garlic clove, finely chopped
300 g/10½ oz. cooked vermicelli rice noodles
15 g/½ oz. dill, roughly chopped
black pepper

MARINADE
1 tbsp fish sauce
1 tsp light brown sugar
½ tsp grated fresh root ginger
½ tsp ground turmeric

DRESSING
1 tbsp fish sauce
1 lime, juice
2 tsp light brown sugar
½ birds-eye red chilli/chile, finely sliced
1 tbsp water

SERVES 2

TAKES 30 MINUTES

First make the marinade. In a mixing bowl, stir together the fish sauce, sugar, ginger and turmeric. Add the fish and a good grind of black pepper. Toss together and set aside. (See Tip, below.)

Meanwhile, make the dressing by mixing all the ingredients in a small bowl. Set aside.

Heat the oil in a large frying pan/skillet over a medium-high heat. When it's hot, fry the marinated fish for 4 minutes, stirring occasionally, but allowing the pieces to take on a little colour. Lift out of the pan and set aside on a plate.

Add the onion and green beans to the pan and fry for 4 minutes (you may need to lower the heat a touch if they brown too quickly). Add the garlic and fry, stirring regularly, for another 4 minutes until all the vegetables are tender and a little golden. Tip the fish back into the pan and stir for a minute or two to reheat.

Take the pan off the heat. Tip in the noodles and add most of the dressing and most of the dill to the pan then gently toss everything together. Divide between serving plates, spoon over the remaining dressing and scatter with the remaining dill to serve.

TIP: *If you have time, ideally marinade the monkfish for 20 minutes prior to cooking.*

STEAK SALAD WITH RANCH-STYLE DRESSING

Bavette is a typically inexpensive cut of steak, taken from the flank or skirt, that is quite lean but extremely flavoursome. It's perfect in this summery steak salad, which is best served somewhere between warm and room temperature.

2 x 150-g/5½-oz. bavette/ flap steaks
400 g/14 oz. waxy new potatoes (I like La Ratte), halved lengthways
2 tbsp olive oil
4 garlic cloves, unpeeled
4-5 thyme sprigs
2 corn on the cob
80 g/3 oz. wild rocket/arugula leaves
salt and black pepper

RANCH-STYLE DRESSING
4 tbsp Greek-style yogurt
3 tbsp mayonnaise
1 tbsp white wine vinegar
1 heaped tsp dried dill

SERVES 2

TAKES 30 MINUTES

Preheat the oven to 220°C/200°C fan/425°F/Gas 7.

Take the steaks out of their packaging and season all over with salt and pepper; set aside until ready to cook.

Toss the potatoes with 1 tablespoon oil, the garlic cloves and thyme, spread over a roasting tray and roast for 10 minutes.

Meanwhile, mix all the dressing ingredients and season well with salt and pepper.

Stir the potatoes. Brush the corn all over with ½ tablespoon oil, season with a little salt and add to the tray with the potatoes. Roast for a final 15 minutes.

Heat a barbecue, griddle or frying pan/skillet to a high heat. Brush the steaks with the remaining ½ tablespoon oil and cook for about 2–3 minutes on each side for medium rare. If they are thick, you may need to give them a bit longer.

Set the steaks aside to rest for 5 minutes. Also let the potatoes and sweetcorn cool for 5 minutes once out of the oven.

Use a knife to cut the kernels from the corn (see Tip). Divide the rocket leaves between plates, scatter over the potatoes, garlic cloves and sweetcorn. Slice the steaks and arrange on top, then drizzle with the dressing (you may not need it all). Serve immediately.

TIP: *To remove the kernels from the cobs, place the cobs upright on a chopping board. Use a sharp knife to shear the kernels from the cob using downward strokes.*

CHICKEN SCHNITTIES WITH BROCCOLI & BACON SLAW

Schnitzel is one of those universally loved meals, and this recipe works just as well with turkey, pork or veal. In fact, some supermarkets sell pre-bashed escalopes which makes the whole process even quicker. I think schnitzel is best served with a saucy slaw, and this one is as good as it gets. If you plan to double the recipe, then it's quickest to use a food processor to pulse the broccoli.

2 x 150-g/5½-oz. chicken breasts
3 tbsp plain/all-purpose flour
1 egg
½ tsp garlic granules
50 g/½ cup panko breadcrumbs
2 tbsp sesame seeds (optional)
3 tbsp vegetable or sunflower oil
salt and black pepper
lemon wedges, to serve

BROCCOLI & BACON SLAW
4 rashers/slices smoked streaky/fatty bacon
150 g/5½ oz. broccoli florets
2½ tbsp mayonnaise
2½ tbsp Greek-style yogurt
1 scant tsp hot horseradish
squeeze of lemon juice, plus wedges to serve
2 tbsp dried cranberries, roughly chopped
2 tbsp finely diced red onion
2 tbsp sunflower seeds

SERVES 2

TAKES 35 MINUTES

For the slaw, chop the bacon into small strips. Add to a large frying pan/skillet (no oil required), set over medium heat, and fry until golden, about 5 minutes. Set aside.

Meanwhile, with your hands, break the raw broccoli florets into tiny pieces, roughly the size of your little finger tip. (Or, for speed, roughly pulse in a food processor or roughly chop with a knife.)

In a mixing bowl, stir together the mayonnaise, yogurt, horseradish and lemon juice and season with salt and pepper. Toss in the bacon, broccoli, cranberries, onion and sunflower seeds; mix together, season to taste and set aside.

For the schnitzels, place the chicken breasts between 2 sheets of parchment paper and use a rolling pin to bash to an even thickness (about 5mm–1 cm/¼–½ inch). Season with salt and pepper.

Tip the flour onto a plate. Beat the egg and garlic granules in a wide, shallow bowl. Mix the panko, sesame seeds (if using) and a pinch of salt on a third plate. One at a time, coat the chicken breasts in the flour, then the egg and finally the breadcrumbs.

Heat the oil in the frying pan over a medium heat. Fry the schnitzels for about 5 minutes on each side, or until cooked through. Serve with the slaw and lemon wedges for squeezing.

POMEGRANATE-GLAZED LAMB & FETA SALAD

At its heart, this is really just a Greek salad with a beautiful, quick-marinated piece of lamb on top, and some pomegranate seeds for tang. I honestly can't think of anything better to eat on a warm evening.

2 tbsp extra virgin olive oil
1½ tbsp pomegranate molasses
1½ tbsp balsamic vinegar
1 garlic clove, crushed
2 x 150-g/5½-oz. lamb rump steaks

SALAD
1 head romaine or cos lettuce
150 g/5½ oz. cucumber
150 g/5½ oz. cherry tomatoes
½ red onion
80 g/3 oz. feta, cubed or crumbled
50 g/2 oz. pomegranate seeds
handful flat-leaf parsley, roughly chopped

SERVES 2

TAKES 25 MINUTES

Mix ½ tablespoon olive oil, ½ tablespoon pomegranate molasses and ½ tablespoon balsamic vinegar with the garlic. Season with salt and pepper and add the lamb steaks, turning to coat them. Set aside, while you prepare the salad.

Chop the lettuce and cucumber into bite-size pieces, halve the tomatoes and thinly slice the onion; toss everything in a bowl. Mix the feta, pomegranate seeds and parsley with ½ tablespoon olive oil and then scatter over the top.

Preheat a griddle pan over a high heat. Cook the lamb steaks for 4 minutes on each side, or until cooked through but still a little pink in the middle. (You could also cook them for the same time under a hot grill/broiler or on a barbecue.) Rest for 5 minutes.

Stir together the remaining 1 tablespoon oil, 1 tablespoon pomegranate molasses and 1 tablespoon balsamic vinegar. Add any resting juices from the lamb to the mixture, season and drizzle over the salad. Slice the meat and serve on top.

ORZO CHICKEN PICCATA

Chicken piccata is an Italian-American dish that brings together a very happy combination of ingredients - butter, lemon juice and capers - for a rich sauce cut with plenty of acidity and saltiness.

2 skinless and boneless chicken breasts (about 320-g/11½ oz. total weight)
2 tbsp plain/all-purpose flour
1 tbsp olive oil
50 g/3½ tbsp unsalted butter
1 echalion shallot, finely diced
2 tbsp nonpareille capers, drained
½ lemon, juice
150 g/¾ cup dried orzo
300 g/10½ oz. fresh leaf spinach
20 g/scant ⅓ cup finely grated Parmesan
salt and black pepper

SERVES 2

TAKES 30 MINUTES

Place the chicken breasts between 2 sheets of parchment and use a rolling pin to bash to an even thickness (about 1 cm/½ inch). Season with salt and pepper, then dust all over with the flour.

Heat the oil in a large frying pan/skillet over a high heat. Fry the chicken for 2–3 minutes on each side, then lift out of the pan and set aside on a plate.

Turn the heat under the pan to medium-high, add the butter, shallot, capers and a pinch of salt and fry for 2–3 minutes. Squeeze in the lemon juice, then return the chicken to the pan and cook gently for a final 3–4 minutes, or until cooked through.

Meanwhile, bring a large saucepan of salted water to the boil. Cook the orzo for 1 minute less than the pack instructions, then drain.

Spoon the chicken and about three quarters of the sauce onto the plate and cover with a sheet of foil to keep warm. Turn the heat under the pan to high and add the spinach, cooking until wilted and the excess liquid has bubbled off.

Tip the drained orzo and the Parmesan into the pan and stir with the spinach. Divide between plates and top with the chicken and sauce.

GOCHUJANG PORK & AUBERGINE

I tried various methods for cooking the aubergine in this dish and grilling seems to be the quickest and most effective. It also means you can get on with frying the pork while it cooks. This is absolutely packed with flavour and offers a highly satisfying meal in less than 30 minutes.

2 aubergines/eggplants, sliced into half-moons about 5 mm/¼ inch thick
3 tbsp vegetable or sunflower oil
1 small onion, finely diced
2 garlic cloves, finely grated or crushed
1 tsp finely grated fresh root ginger
500 g/1 lb. 2 oz. minced/ground pork (about 8% fat)
15 g/½ oz. Thai basil, leaves picked and torn

GOCHUJANG SAUCE
3 tbsp gochujang paste
2 tbsp soy sauce
2 tbsp Shaoxing rice wine
1 tbsp honey

TO SERVE
steamed rice or noodles
toasted sesame oil
toasted sesame seeds

SERVES 4

TAKES 30 MINUTES

Preheat the grill/broiler to high (280°C/536°F) and line your largest oven tray with foil. Toss the aubergine half-moons with 2 tablespoons oil, then arrange on the tray in a single layer. Grill/broil for about 6 minutes on each side until they are golden.

Meanwhile, heat the remaining 1 tablespoon oil in a large frying pan/skillet over a medium-high heat. Stir-fry the onion, garlic and ginger for 2–3 minutes until fragrant. Add the pork and fry for 6–7 minutes until any excess liquid has bubbled off from the pan and the pork is starting to turn golden.

Mix the sauce ingredients with 3 tablespoons water, then tip into the pan. Add the cooked aubergine and stir everything over the heat until warmed through and nicely coated. Top with the basil leaves, then serve with rice or noodles. You can drizzle the pork with a little toasted sesame oil and scatter with toasted sesame seeds too, if you like.

CHICKEN BURGERS WITH KIMCHI SLAW

This is my kind of burger: zingy, cheesy and with plenty of crunchy, punchy slaw. Chicken breasts come in all sizes. I like to bash them to even out the thickness, and then cut into two pieces so they cook quickly and stack neatly in the buns.

1 tsp toasted sesame oil
1 heaped tbsp gochujang paste
1 tbsp soy sauce
2 garlic cloves, crushed
4 small chicken breasts (about 150 g/5½ oz. each)
salt and black pepper

KIMCHI SLAW
½ small white cabbage (about 400 g/14 oz.), finely sliced or shredded
½ red onion, thinly sliced
4 tbsp mayonnaise, plus extra to serve
4 tbsp kimchi (I like Vadasz)

TO SERVE
4 brioche burger buns, split
8 slices Cheddar
4 lettuce leaves

SERVES 4

TAKES 30 MINUTES, plus marinating

Mix the sesame oil, gochujang, soy sauce and garlic in a resealable food bag or non-reactive mixing bowl. Place the chicken breasts between 2 sheets of parchment paper and use a rolling pin to bash to an even thickness (about 1 cm/½ inch). Then slice each one in half, to make 8 even-ish pieces, and stir into the marinade and season with a little salt and pepper. Set aside to marinate for at least 20 minutes and up to 12 hours.

For the kimchi slaw, mix all the ingredients with a pinch of salt. This can be done up to 2 hours in advance.

Heat a frying pan/skillet or griddle over a high heat. Gently toast the buns and set aside. Next, cook the chicken fillets for 3 minutes on one side, then turn and cook for a couple of minutes before topping them with slices of cheese. Cook for another 2 minutes until the chicken is cooked through and the cheese has melted.

Spread the bun bases with a little mayonnaise. Top with a lettuce leaf, then 2 pieces of chicken, and a good heap of the slaw. Finish with the bun lids and serve immediately.

CHIPOTLE-ORANGE PORK TACOS

I love a meal where you can simply place everything on the table and let everyone feed themselves. The chipotle pork is the star of the show here, but you could also use chicken thigh fillets.

1 small red onion, thinly sliced
1 lime, juice
pinch of ground cumin
150 g/½ cup soured cream
12 small corn tortillas
2 avocados, sliced
100 g/1 cup grated Cheddar cheese
salt and black pepper

CHIPOTLE-ORANGE PORK
2 tbsp chipotle chilli paste (I like Gran Luchito)
½ orange or 1 satsuma, juice
2 garlic cloves, crushed
4 pork shoulder steaks (about 650 g/1½ lb.)

SERVES 4

TAKES 35 MINUTES plus marinating

Start by marinating the pork. Mix the chipotle paste, orange juice, garlic and a pinch of salt in a resealable food bag or non-reactive mixing bowl. Add the pork and mix to coat in the marinade. This can be cooked straightaway or marinated for up to 2 hours.

Place the red onion in a small bowl, add a pinch of salt and squeeze over the lime juice. Toss to combine and set aside for 10 minutes, or up to 1 hour, tossing occasionally.

Preheat the grill/broiler to high; arrange a rack on the top shelf. Lay the pork steaks out on a foil-lined tray. Grill/broil for 6–7 minutes on each side until cooked through and nicely charred in places. Rest for 5 minutes.

In a small bowl, mix a pinch of ground cumin and a pinch of salt into the soured cream.

While the pork is resting, in a dry frying pan/skillet set over a medium-high heat, warm the tortillas for about 30 seconds–1 minute on each side. Wrap them in a clean kitchen towel to keep them warm as you go.

Slice the pork, spooning over any of the cooking juices. Place on the table with the red onions, soured cream, sliced avocados, grated Cheddar and warm tortillas and invite everyone to build their own tacos.

PACKED WITH PLANTS

WHOLESOME

& COLOURFUL

PLANT-POWERED

RECIPES.

ROASTED RICE & TOFU SALAD

Most viral recipes don't look worth the bother, but having seen lots of roasted Thai-style rice salads I decided to give it a go. Fortunately, it was well worth it.

½ tbsp vegetable or sunflower oil
150 g/5½ oz. firm tofu, cut into cubes and patted dry
1 large echalion shallot, halved and thinly sliced
250-g/9-oz. pouch cooked jasmine rice
1 heaped tbsp Thai red curry paste (vegan, if desired)
50 g/⅓ cup cashews
100 g/3½ oz. cucumber, halved and thinly sliced
100 g/3½ oz. white or red cabbage, finely shredded
handful coriander/cilantro and mint leaves, shredded
salt

DRESSING
1 lime, juice
2 tsp fish sauce (use a vegan alternative, if desired, or soy sauce)
1 tsp maple syrup

SERVES 2

TAKES 35 MINUTES

PLANT POINTS 7

Preheat the oven to 220°C/200°C fan/425°F/Gas 7.

Toss the oil in a large mixing bowl with the tofu and about two thirds of the shallot. Heat the rice in the microwave according to the pack instructions, then add to the bowl, along with the curry paste and a pinch of salt. Toss everything together.

Spread over a roasting tray and roast for 20 minutes, stirring halfway. On a separate tray, add the cashews to the oven for the last 7 minutes. Take everything out and cool for 5 minutes.

Meanwhile, rinse out the mixing bowl and add the cucumber, cabbage and remaining shallot.

In a separate small bowl combine the dressing ingredients.

Add the rice and tofu, cashews and herbs to the mixing bowl. Pour in the dressing, toss everything together and serve immediately.

TRAYBAKED SQUASH, HALLOUMI & QUINOA

An exemplary traybake recipe, ticking every box in terms of texture, flavour and colour. Roasting quinoa is a revelation, giving it a nice bit of crunch.

1 butternut squash, peeled, deseeded and cut into 2.5 cm/1-inch chunks
5 garlic cloves, unpeeled
3 tbsp olive oil
250-g/9-oz. pouch cooked quinoa
200 g/7oz. long-stem broccoli, trimmed
2 x 225-g/8-oz. packs halloumi, cut into 2.5 cm/1-inch chunks
1 lemon, juice
25 g/¼ cup pumpkin seeds
1 tsp honey
1 mild red chilli/chile, deseeded and finely diced

SERVES 4
TAKES 50 MINUTES
PLANT POINTS 6½

Preheat the oven to 220°C/200°C fan/425°F/Gas 7.

Toss the squash and garlic cloves with 1 tablespoon oil and some salt and pepper, then spread out over your largest roasting tray. Roast for 20–25 minutes, stirring halfway, until turning golden.

Take the tray out of the oven and remove and set aside the garlic cloves. Add the quinoa, broccoli and halloumi to the tray, drizzle over another 1 tablespoon oil and the juice of half a lemon. Season with a little more salt and pepper and stir everything together. Scatter over the pumpkin seeds and roast everything for a final 15 minutes.

Meanwhile, discard the skin from the roasted garlic and mash the caramelized cloves in a bowl. Whisk in the remaining 1 tablespoon oil, juice of half lemon, honey and diced chilli and season.

Remove the tray of vegetables from the oven and spoon over the dressing. Divide between plates to serve.

CRUNCHY SLAW WITH TAHINI-LIME DRESSING

This adaptable salad is really all about the dressing. Change up the vegetables as you please, and add cooked prawns, roasted chickpeas or shredded chicken.

150 g/5½ oz. shredded red cabbage (use a mandolin, if you have one)
100 g/3½ oz. mangetout/snow peas, sliced
1 large carrot, grated
½ small red onion, finely sliced
1 yellow, red or orange (bell) pepper, deseeded and sliced
2 tbsp roasted cashews, roughly chopped

TAHINI-LIME DRESSING
3 tbsp tahini
1 lime, juice
1 tbsp soy sauce
1 tsp maple syrup
1 small garlic clove, finely grated

SERVES 2

TAKES 15 MINUTES

PLANT POINTS 6½

Start by making the dressing. Whisk together the tahini, lime juice, soy sauce, maple syrup and garlic in a bowl. Add 1–2 tablespoons water, a little at a time (tahini varies in consistency, so you may need more or less), until you have smooth dressing about the consistency of single/light cream. Taste and add a pinch of salt or more lime juice, if needed.

Throw all of the vegetables into a large mixing bowl. Add the dressing and toss everything together. Serve, with or without extra protein (see recipe introduction).

MISO AUBERGINE & SILKEN TOFU

Roast the aubergine in advance for a quick and impressive plant-based meal.

3 aubergines/eggplants
3 tbsp sunflower oil
4 spring onions/scallions, chopped and whites and greens separated
2 garlic cloves, finely chopped
15 g/½ oz. fresh root ginger, peeled and cut into thin matchsticks
300-g/10½-oz. pack silken tofu
1 red chilli/chile, sliced
salt
brown rice, to serve

MISO SAUCE
2 tbsp white miso paste
2 tbsp Shaoxing rice wine
2 tbsp maple syrup
1 tbsp soy sauce
2 tsp rice vinegar

SERVES 3

TAKES 1 HOUR

PLANT POINTS 5

Preheat the oven to 220°C/200°C fan/425°F/Gas 7. Take each aubergine and slice into it from base to root at 1-cm/½-inch intervals. Brush inside and outside with 2 tablespoons oil and season inside the cuts lightly with salt. Lay on a parchment paper-lined baking tray. Roast for 40–50 minutes, turning halfway, until golden and tender. Mix the sauce ingredients and 2 tablespoons water in a bowl. Put the tofu on paper towel to absorb liquid.

In a large frying pan/skillet, heat the remaining oil over a medium-high heat. Fry the spring onion whites, garlic and ginger for 2–3 minutes, add the sauce and bubble for 1 minute. Nestle the aubergines into the sauce, turning them once so they're coated and simmer for 1 minute. Chop the tofu and tumble it over the top. Take off the heat and scatter with the spring onion greens and red chilli. Serve with rice.

Pictured on pages 110–111

CHARRED HARISSA-YOGURT SALMON WITH CORN TABBOULEH

A quick yogurt and harissa marinade transforms a large fillet of salmon into a bold centrepiece. Paired with a vibrant bulgur salad, which has its roots in tabbouleh, this makes a quick and highly satisfying supper.

500-g/1 lb. 2-oz. salmon fillet
100 g/scant ½ cup Greek-style yogurt
2 heaped tbsp harissa
2 garlic cloves, crushed
salt and black pepper

BULGUR SALAD
200 g/1 cup bulgur wheat, rinsed
2 corn on the cob
2 tbsp extra virgin olive oil
2 tbsp lemon juice
scant ½ tsp ground allspice
4 spring onions/scallions, finely chopped
100 g/3½ oz. radishes, trimmed and sliced
handful mint leaves, roughly chopped

SERVES 4
TAKES 20 MINUTES
PLANT POINTS 5½

Preheat the grill/broiler to high; place a rack on the top shelf. Place the salmon, skin-side down, on a foil-lined baking tray. Slash the fillet 2–3 times in its thickest section to help it cook evenly, then season all over with salt and pepper.

Mix the yogurt, harissa and garlic and spread all over the salmon. Grill for 10–12 minutes until cooked through (lower the rack if it starts catching).

Meanwhile, bring a large saucepan of salted boiling water to the boil. Add the bulgur and corn cobs and boil for 6 minutes.

Meanwhile, whisk the oil, lemon juice, allspice and a large pinch of salt in a mixing bowl.

Drain the bulgur and set aside the sweetcorn. Tip the hot bulgur into the dressing and toss together. Slice the sweetcorn off the cobs (see Tip, page 88) and tip into the bowl of bulgur, also adding the spring onions, radishes and mint. Toss together and divide between serving plates before topping with the flaked salmon.

DRUNKEN GREEN NOODLES

There are several theories on how Thai drunken noodles got their name: some suggest it's the perfect plate to eat after a night out, others say the dish is so spicy it must be accompanied by an ice-cold beer. I tend to go a little easy on the chilli/chile, usually adding half a bird's eye for a middling kick, but do add more if so desired. As with any stir-fry recipe, once you start cooking everything happens very quickly, so make sure all your ingredients are prepped and ready to go.

150 g/5$\frac{1}{2}$ oz. dried flat rice noodles
about 300 g/10$\frac{1}{2}$ oz. mixed green veg (I use a mix of asparagus, pak choi/bok choy and long-stem broccoli)
2 tbsp vegetable oil
1 small onion, halved and sliced
2 garlic cloves, sliced
1 tsp finely grated fresh root ginger
$\frac{1}{2}$–1 bird's eye chilli/chile, thinly sliced
about 15 g/$\frac{1}{2}$ oz. Thai basil, leaves picked
1 lime, juice of $\frac{1}{2}$ and the rest in wedges
30 g/$\frac{1}{4}$ cup roasted cashews, chopped

SAUCE
1 tbsp soy sauce
1 tbsp oyster sauce
2 tsp fish sauce
1$\frac{1}{2}$ tsp soft light brown sugar

SERVES 2
TAKES 25 MINUTES
PLANT POINTS 7$\frac{1}{2}$

Place the noodles in a large heatproof bowl, cover with just-boiled water and let soak for 6–7 minutes. Drain and rinse under the cold tap, then shake dry and set aside.

Meanwhile in a small bowl mix the sauce ingredients with 1 tablespoon water.

Next, prepare the green vegetables by chopping them into generous bite-size pieces.

When everything is prepared, start cooking. Heat the oil in a large wok or frying pan/skillet over a high heat. When hot, fry the onion, garlic and ginger for 1 minute, then tip in the green vegetables and stir-fry for 2–3 minutes.

Tip in the chilli and basil leaves and fry for 30 seconds, then add the noodles and the sauce and toss over the heat for minute until piping hot. Squeeze over the juice of half a lime, then divide between serving plates.

Scatter with the cashews and serve with extra lime wedges on the side for squeezing.

BEETROOT & ARTICHOKE SOUP WITH ROASTED CHICKPEAS & QUINOA

This soup is soothing, velvety and packed with good things. Jerusalem artichokes are in season from November to March and have a divinely nutty and sweet flavour, plus they are a source of prebiotic fibre.

1 tbsp olive oil
1 tbsp butter
1 large onion, diced
1 leek, roughly chopped
250 g/9 oz. Jerusalem artichokes, peeled and roughly chopped
250 g/9 oz. raw beetroot/beet, peeled and roughly chopped
250 g/9 oz. carrots, peeled and roughly chopped
1 litre/1 quart chicken or vegetable stock
squeeze of lemon juice
salt and black pepper

ROASTED CHICKPEAS & QUINOA
240 g/8½ oz. cooked queen chickpeas from a jar, drained
250-g/9-oz. pouch cooked quinoa
1 tbsp olive oil
2 garlic cloves, unpeeled and bashed
squeeze of lemon juice

SERVES 4

TAKES 45 MINUTES

PLANT POINTS 8½

Preheat the oven to 200°C/180°C fan/400°F/Gas 6.

Heat the oil and the butter in a large saucepan over a medium-high heat. Fry the onion with a good pinch of salt for a couple of minutes, then add the leek and fry for 5 minutes. Add the Jerusalem artichokes, beetroot and carrots with another pinch of salt. Cover and cook for about 10–15 minutes, stirring regularly, until they are starting to soften and caramelize.

Add the stock to the pan, bring to a simmer and cook for about 15–20 minutes, or until all of the vegetables are completely soft. Whizz in a blender with a squeeze of lemon juice and salt and pepper to taste.

Meanwhile, for the topping, pat the chickpeas dry if needed. Toss the chickpeas, quinoa, oil, bashed garlic cloves and lemon juice on a baking tray; season with salt and pepper. Roast for 15–20 minutes, stirring halfway, until golden in places.

Reheat the soup if necessary, then ladle into bowls and scatter with the toasted quinoa and chickpea topping.

A VERY SIMPLE QUESADILLA WITH AVOCADO SOURED CREAM

Oven baking a tray of quesadillas is a simple hack that is far less time consuming (and less messy) than frying them individually. You could certainly double this recipe to efficiently feed a crowd.

1 tbsp olive oil, plus a splash more for brushing
1 red onion, diced
1 red, yellow or green (bell) pepper, deseeded and finely diced
½ tsp salt
100 g/½ cup frozen sweetcorn kernels
240 g/1¼ cups cooked black beans
½ tsp ground cumin
½ tsp hot or regular smoked paprika
½ lime, juice
100 g/1 cup grated mature/sharp Cheddar
4 large, seeded tortilla wraps

AVOCADO SOURED CREAM
2 ripe avocados
4 tbsp soured cream
½ lime, juice
handful coriander/cilantro leaves, chopped
salt

SERVES 4

TAKES 20 MINUTES

PLANT POINTS 7¼

Preheat the oven to 220°C/200°C fan/425°F/Gas 7; line your largest baking tray with foil.

Heat the oil in a large frying pan/skillet over a medium-high heat. Fry the onion, pepper and salt for 4–5 minutes. Add the sweetcorn and beans and fry for 2–3 minutes more, then stir in the spices and cook out for a minute. Squeeze in the lime juice and take the pan off the heat.

Brush one side of the tortillas with a little oil and place the oiled-side down on the foil. Divide the bean mixture equally between the tortillas, covering only one half and mashing it down a little with a fork. Sprinkle the cheese over the filling, then fold the tortillas in half to make semi-circles. Bake for 5 minutes.

Meanwhile mash the avocado flesh with a fork, then mix with the soured cream, lime juice, coriander and a good pinch of salt.

When the tortillas come out of the oven, allow to cool for a couple of minutes, then halve them and serve with the avocado soured cream on the side.

ROASTED ROOTS & LENTILS WITH DATE & CAPER DRESSING

You can mix up the root vegetables in this salad, but carrot and parsnips look great and have an earthy sweetness about them.

300 g/10½ oz. carrots and parsnips, scrubbed, trimmed and halved lengthways
4 tbsp olive oil
1 tsp ground coriander
1 large echalion shallot, sliced
2 medjool dates, pitted and roughly chopped
2 tbsp nonpareille capers, rinsed
1½–2 tbsp cider vinegar
400-g/14-oz. can cooked beluga lentils, drained
handful mint leaves, shredded
75 g/3 oz. goat's cheese, crumbled
salt and black pepper

SERVES 2

TAKES 40 MINUTES

PLANT POINTS 6¾

Preheat the oven to 220°C/200°C fan/425°F/Gas 7.

Toss the carrots and parsnips with 1 tablespoon oil, the ground coriander and a good pinch of salt. Scatter over a parchment paper-lined roasting tray and roast for 25–30 minutes, turning halfway, until golden and tender.

Heat the remaining 3 tablespoons oil in a large frying pan/skillet over a medium heat. Fry the shallot with a pinch of salt for 5 minutes until softened, then add the dates and capers and fry for a minute more. Splash in the vinegar, then stir in the lentils. Check the seasoning, adding salt and pepper or more vinegar to taste.

Arrange the lentils over plates and top with the roasted roots. Scatter with the mint and goat's cheese, and serve.

WHAT'S IN THE KITCHEN?

NO TIME TO SHOP? CLEVER RECIPES TO RUSTLE UP FROM A WELL-STOCKED CUPBOARD.

FIERY EGGS

Shakshuka seems to have captured the brunch zeitgeist in the last decade, but this southern Italian dish (known as 'eggs in purgatory') is far easier to make, just as delicious, and requires ingredients that are almost certainly already in the cupboard at home.

2 tbsp extra virgin olive oil
2 garlic cloves, crushed or finely grated
pinch of chilli/hot red pepper flakes
400-g/14-oz. can finely chopped tomatoes
pinch of sugar (optional)
4 eggs
Parmesan, for grating
salt and black pepper

TO SERVE
Parmesan, for grating
basil leaves (optional)
crusty bread

SERVES 2

TAKES 20 MINUTES

Heat the oil over a medium-high heat in a large frying pan/skillet. Add the garlic and a pinch of salt and fry for a minute until you can smell the garlic.

Stir in the chilli flakes and then add the tomatoes. Add a pinch more salt and allow to simmer gently for about 8–10 minutes until the sauce has thickened. Taste and add more salt, chilli or a pinch of sugar if it needs it.

Use the back of a spoon to make 4 indents in the sauce and crack an egg into each. Cook for 5–6 minutes or until the whites are cooked and yolks are set but still soft. (Use a fork to gently pull the uncooked whites into the sauce so they cook a bit more quickly and cover the pan with a lid briefly at the end of cooking if the tops of the yolks require a little help to set.)

Top with grated Parmesan (and fresh basil leaves if you have them), grind over a little black pepper and serve with plenty of crusty bread.

SICILIAN-STYLE TUNA PASTA

It never ceases to amaze me how such an elegant plate of food can be produced from storecupboard ingredients.

200 g/7 oz. dried spaghetti
220-g/8-oz. jar tuna in olive oil
1 echalion shallot (or 1/2 onion), finely chopped
2 garlic cloves, finely chopped
1 tbsp nonpareille capers
20 pitted kalamata olives, halved
large pinch of chilli/hot red pepper flakes
1 unwaxed lemon, zest and juice (optional)
salt
grated Parmesan, to serve
chopped flat-leaf parsley, to garnish (optional)

SERVES 2

TAKES 20 MINUTES

Bring a large pan of salted water to the boil and cook the spaghetti for 1 minute less than the pack instructions. Scoop out a mugful of the pasta cooking water before draining the spaghetti.

Meanwhile, empty the oil from the jar of tuna into in a large frying pan/skillet and set over a medium-high heat. Fry the shallot with a pinch of salt for 2 minutes, then add the garlic, capers and olives. Fry for another 2–3 minutes, then roughly flake in the tuna and add the chilli flakes, stirring over the heat for a moment. If you're using the lemon zest add it now too.

Add the drained pasta to the pan, along with a glug of the reserved cooking water and the lemon juice, if using. Toss over the heat for a minute, and divide between plates. Serve with grated Parmesan, if liked.

JAMMY BUTTERY TOMATO SAUCE

This is an adaptation of Marcella Hazan's 'Tomato Sauce with Onion and Butter'. I think this particular recipe is life-changing, you won't make tomato sauce another way again.

400-g/14-oz. can peeled tomatoes (ideally San Marzano)
1/2 tsp salt
2 garlic cloves, unpeeled and bashed
1 small onion, unpeeled and halved
40 g/2 1/2 tbsp unsalted butter, cut into three pieces

SERVES 2–3

TAKES 50 MINUTES

Preheat the oven to 200°C/180°C fan/400°F/Gas 6. Tip the tomatoes into a medium baking dish (about 1.5 litres/6 cups in volume) and roughly chop them with a cutlery knife. Stir in the salt and garlic cloves.

Press the onion halves, cut-side down, into the tomato mixture and scatter the pieces of butter around them. Bake for 40–45 minutes, stirring halfway. If there are some charred bits around the edges, stir them back in.

When the sauce is ready, remove and discard the onion halves. Discard the skin from the garlic cloves and mash the flesh with a fork into the sauce. Also mash any larger chunks of tomato. Stir and serve with cooked pasta.

Pictured on pages 128–129

BAKED TOMATO RICE WITH HALLOUMI & BUTTER BEANS

I adore baked rice dishes, there's something so pleasing about how the grains soak up all the flavours of the other ingredients as they cook. Packs of halloumi will keep in the fridge for about 9 months, so it has become a bit of a 'storecupboard hero' ingredient for me, a handy protein source to fall back on when I haven't had time to go to the shops. Serve a crisp green salad alongside this if you wish.

200 g/1 cup white basmati rice, well rinsed
6 sundried tomatoes in oil, chopped, plus 2½ tbsp of the oil
1 large red onion, finely diced
¾ tsp salt
2 garlic cloves, finely chopped
1 tsp sweet smoked paprika
1 tbsp tomato purée/paste
240 g/8½ oz. cooked butter beans (or black beans, or chickpeas)
500 ml/2 cups chicken or vegetable stock
½ lemon, thinly sliced
250-g/9-oz. block halloumi, drained and cut into 2.5 cm-1-inch chunks

SERVES 4

TAKES 1 HOUR

Preheat the oven to 200°C/180°C fan/400°F/Gas 6. Soak the rinsed rice in a bowl of cold water.

Meanwhile, heat 2 tablespoons oil from the sundried tomatoes in an ovenproof frying pan/skillet (about 28 cm/ 11 inches in diameter) over a medium-high heat. Fry the onion and garlic with ½ teaspoon salt for 3–4 minutes, then add the sundried tomatoes and cook for another 3–4 minutes. Add the paprika and tomato purée and fry, stirring, for another minute.

Drain the rice thoroughly and add to the pan along with the butter beans and the remaining ¼ teaspoon salt. Fry for a couple of minutes and don't worry if the rice sticks to the bottom of the pan a bit.

Pour in the stock and bring everything to a simmer. Scatter the sliced lemons over the top, then transfer the pan to the oven. Bake for 20 minutes.

Take the pan out of the oven and scatter the diced halloumi over the top, nudging the chunks gently into the rice. Return to the oven for another 15–20 minutes until the rice is crisp on top and the halloumi is turning golden. Allow to stand for 5 minutes before serving with a green salad, if liked.

STICKY GYOZA UDON

I couldn't survive weeknight cooking without frozen dumplings. They save me at least once a week, added to soy-spiked soups, served over crunchy Asian-style slaw or tossed in a quick pan of noodles for one. I usually have cabbage, too. It's an inexpensive and versatile vegetable that lasts for ages in the fridge and works its way into all kinds of meals. That said, if you don't have any, feel free to leave it out.

½ tbsp sunflower or vegetable oil
3–5 frozen dumplings (I like Itsu chicken gyoza)
100 g/3½ oz. savoy cabbage, roughly chopped
150 g/5½ oz. ready-to-cook udon noodles
1 spring onion/scallion, chopped

SAUCE
2 tsp soy sauce
2 tsp oyster sauce
1 tsp cider vinegar
½ tsp hot honey (or regular honey)
½ tsp toasted sesame oil

SERVES 1

TAKES 15 MINUTES

Heat the oil in a medium frying pan/skillet over a medium heat. Add the dumplings and the cabbage and cook for 3–4 minutes. Don't move the dumplings so they get a crispy bottom, but stir the cabbage a little so it cooks evenly.

Meanwhile mix the sauce ingredients and 1 teaspoon water in a small bowl.

Add 2 tablespoons water to the pan with the dumplings, lower the heat, cover with a lid and steam for 2–3 minutes. At the same time, place the udon noodles in a heatproof bowl and cover with just-boiled water from the kettle, soaking for 2–3 minutes.

Drain the noodles and tip into the pan along with sauce. Turn the heat up, and toss everything together until coated. Serve scattered with the spring onions.

TURMERIC-FRIED QUINOA WITH SMOKED MACKEREL

This has all the comforting flavours of a classic kedgeree, with the added nuttiness of quinoa (though you could easily swap in a packet of cooked rice). It's quick, convenient, and made with ingredients I almost always have at home (sometimes swapping canned mackerel for smoked). For an extra boost of veg, toss a handful of frozen peas in with the quinoa.

2 eggs
1 tbsp olive oil
1 tbsp unsalted butter
1 onion, finely diced
½ tsp salt
1 tsp medium curry powder
½ tsp ground turmeric
3 cardamom pods (optional)
250-g/9-oz. pouch cooked quinoa
½ lemon, juice
180 g/6½ oz. smoked mackerel
black pepper
flat-leaf parsley, to garnish
2 hard-boiled/hard-cooked eggs, to serve (optional)

SERVES 2

TAKES 20 MINUTES

Bring a small saucepan of water to the boil, lower in the eggs and cook for 7 minutes. Then drain and leave to cool in cold water.

Meanwhile, heat the oil and butter in a medium frying pan/skillet over a medium heat. Fry the onion with the salt for 8–10 minutes until soft, then add the spices and fry for another 1–2 minutes.

Add the quinoa and lemon juice and grind over some black pepper, then stir over the heat for a couple of minutes until everything is piping hot.

Take the pan off the heat. Flake in the mackerel, discarding the skin, and toss everything together. Taste and add more lemon juice if needed. Divide between serving plates (remove the cardamom pods, if using) and top with the peeled and quartered eggs. Some chopped flat-leaf parsley is a nice addition.

STIR-FRIED GARLIC & CHILLI PRAWNS

I always have prawns in the freezer. They defrost quickly and can be on-hand for a zingy last-minute supper, like this. I also have edamame beans in the freezer, but you could swap them for another green vegetable if you like, such as broccoli.

160 g/1½ cups frozen edamame
165 g/1 generous cup raw king prawns/jumbo shrimp (defrosted, if frozen)
1 tbsp vegetable or sunflower oil
2 garlic cloves, finely chopped
noodles or rice, to serve

CHILLI SAUCE
2 tsp tomato purée/paste
1 tsp sriracha (or any chilli/hot sauce)
1 tsp soy sauce
1 tsp vinegar (rice if you have it, or wine or cider will do)
1 tsp honey
1 tsp toasted sesame oil

SERVES 2

TAKES 15 MINUTES

Place the edamame in a heatproof bowl and cover with just-boiled water from the kettle. This thaws them before cooking. Pat the prawns dry on paper towels.

In a small bowl mix the sauce ingredients together with 2 teaspoons water.

Heat a medium frying pan/skillet over a high heat. When smoking hot, add the oil and garlic and stir-fry for 30 seconds. Add the prawns and fry for 1 minute more. Tip in the edamame and give everything a stir.

Add the chilli sauce and stir over the heat for a minute or two until everything is nicely coated and the prawns are cooked through. Serve with cooked noodles or rice.

BROTHY PEAS, PASTA & PARMESAN

Here is a one-person recipe constructed from ingredients that I almost always have in my kitchen. Containing two of your five a day, it feels good while providing solace on evenings when energy is running low. The broth is a key player here, so make sure it's good. I keep sachets of Borough Broth's chicken bone broth in my freezer for exactly such purposes.

1 tbsp olive oil
1 small leek, trimmed and finely chopped (or use 1 finely diced onion)
1/4 tsp salt
50 g/2 oz. small dried pasta shapes (I like ditaloni)
80 g/1/2 cup frozen peas
425 ml/1 3/4 cups good-quality bone broth or chicken stock
15 g/scant 1/4 cup finely grated Parmesan, plus extra to serve
black pepper

SERVES 1

TAKES 20 MINUTES

Heat the oil in a medium saucepan over a medium heat. Add the leek and salt, cover with a lid and sweat the leek for 5–6 minutes, stirring regularly, until sweet and softened.

Tip the pasta into the pan and stir over the heat for a minute, then add the peas and bone broth or stock, along with a good grind of black pepper. Simmer for as long as the pasta packet recommends.

When the pasta is cooked to your liking, remove the pan from the heat. Tip in the Parmesan and stir until it melts into the broth. Serve in a big bowl with extra Parmesan on top.

PREP AHEAD

SLOW-COOK,
BATCH-FRIENDLY RECIPES
THAT CAN BE MADE
IN ADVANCE.

LAMB, MEDJOOL & BUTTER BEAN STEW

This is the kind of rich, nourishing and deeply satisfying stew that will see you through winter (not to mention that it packs in about 6 plant varieties). It goes well with couscous, rice or crusty bread, tastes better made a day in advance, and any leftovers will freeze exceptionally well.

1 tbsp olive oil
750 g/1 lb. 10 oz. lamb neck, trimmed of excess fat and cut into large chunks
1 large onion, diced
3 carrots, peeled and roughly chopped
2 garlic cloves, roughly chopped
1 tsp ground allspice
1 cinnamon stick
2 medjool dates, pitted and chopped
200 ml/¾ cup red wine
400-g/14-oz. can chopped tomatoes
500 ml/2 cups chicken stock
400-g/14-oz. can butter beans, rinsed and drained
salt and black pepper
flat-leaf parsley or coriander/ cilantro, to garnish (optional)

SERVES 4–6

TAKES 2 HOURS 30 MINUTES

Preheat the oven to 160°C/140°C fan/320°F/Gas 3.

Heat the oil in a large casserole/Dutch oven over a high heat. Season the lamb all over and add to the pan, leaving it undisturbed for a couple of minutes to seal and brown and then turning and frying for 10 minutes until golden all over. Lift out of the pan and set aside.

Spoon out any excess fat (you want about 1 tablespoon remaining) and fry the onion for a couple of minutes with a large pinch of salt, before adding the carrots and garlic and frying for another 6–8 minutes. Stir in the spices and dates, then add the wine and bubble until reduced by half.

Add the tomatoes and stock, then return the lamb and any juices. Season with salt and pepper, cover with a lid and place in the oven for 45 minutes.

Take the lid off the stew, give it a stir and cook for another 45 minutes. Stir in the butter beans, then cook for another 30 minutes by which point the lamb should be completely tender. If it's not, return to the oven for 30 minutes. Serve scattered with chopped parsley and/or coriander, if you have them.

PULLED ANCHO CHILLI CHICKEN

I cannot take credit for this recipe. It was written by my talented friend and former colleague Myles Williamson many years ago and I have made it regularly since, although this is a much simplified version. I am happy to see that ancho chillies are now widely available in supermarkets and online - they are fruity and mild, and a good choice if feeding kids. You can serve this pulled chicken in tacos, on rice or piled onto a baked sweet potato with grated cheese, soured cream and sliced avocado.

2 tbsp sunflower or vegetable oil
3 red onions, peeled and cut into thin wedges through the root
500 g/1 lb. 2 oz. chicken thigh fillets
3 garlic cloves, crushed
400 g/14 oz. ripe tomatoes, diced (or 400-g/14-oz. can chopped tomatoes)
250 ml/1 cup chicken stock
1 lime, zest and juice

ANCHO SPICE MIX
1 dried ancho chilli/chile or 1 tbsp ancho chilli/chili flakes
1/2 tsp cloves
1/2 tsp fennel seeds
1/2 tbsp soft light brown sugar
1 tsp salt

SERVES 4–6

TAKES 2 HOURS

Preheat the oven to 160°C/140°C fan/320°F/Gas 3.

Heat the oil in a large ovenproof casserole/Dutch oven or sauté pan over a medium-high heat. Fry the onion wedges for 3–4 minutes until starting to take on a little colour.

Meanwhile make the spice mix. If using a whole dried chilli, discard the stem and roughly chop, then add to a small blender or spice grinder with the remaining ingredients. Blend to a powder.

Push the onions to one side and add the chicken to the pan. Leave for a couple of minutes to colour, then turn and cook for 2 minutes more. Add the garlic to the pan and stir everything together. Add the spice mix and fry everything for another 2–3 minutes.

Tip in the tomatoes, stock and lime zest, bring everything to a simmer, cover with a lid and transfer to the oven. Cook for 45 minutes, then remove the lid, stir and cook uncovered for another 45 minutes.

Take the pan out of the oven and cool for 10 minutes. Remove the chicken pieces and shred with 2 forks, then return to the pan. Stir in the lime juice and check the seasoning before serving (see recipe introduction).

SLOW-COOKER CHICKEN NOODLE SOUP

I cannot get through a winter without chicken soup, and there are no real shortcuts to a good one. This is my current favourite. It's roots are in Mexican 'sopa de lima', hence the allspice and lime juice, but I can't help but add noodles and shower it with Parmesan at the end. I get my slow cooker out for this - it's easier than having it on the hob/stovetop and the low, mellow cook ensures great flavour.

CHICKEN BROTH

4 free-range or organic chicken wings
4 free-range or organic chicken drumsticks
1 onion, unpeeled and halved
1 carrot, scrubbed clean and halved
4 garlic cloves, unpeeled
3 tomatoes, roughly chopped
1 tsp salt
8 black peppercorns
6 allspice berries
3 cloves

TO FINISH

1 tbsp olive oil
1 leek, trimmed, halved and thinly sliced
1 carrot, peeled, halved and thinly sliced
200 g/7 oz. broken vermicelli noodles
1 lime, juice
chopped flat-leaf parsley and grated Parmesan, to serve

SERVES 4

TAKES 6–7 HOURS

Preheat the oven to 200°C/180°C fan/400°F/Gas 6.

Place the chicken, onion, carrot and garlic in a roasting tin. Roast for 30 minutes. (You can skip this step, but roasting the chicken really does give the soup a far superior flavour.)

Place the tomatoes, salt, pepper and spices in a slow cooker. Tip in the roasted chicken and vegetables, along with any roasting juices. Add a splash of water to the roasting tin to scrape up any caramelized bits and add these too. Cover with about 1.5 litres/6 cups cold water (depending on the size and depth of your slow cooker or pan you may need more). Cook on low for 5 hours. Alternatively simmer very gently on the hob in a large pot for 2 hours 30 minutes. Turn off the heat and cool for an hour.

Lift the chicken from the broth. Discard the wings and set the drumsticks aside. Strain the broth through a sieve/strainer into bowl, pressing the vegetables to extract as much liquid as possible. Shred the meat from the drumsticks (discard the skin, bones and gristle) and add to the broth. You can also let cool and chill it at this stage.

Heat the oil in a large saucepan over a medium heat. Fry the leek and carrot with a pinch of salt for 5–6 minutes until softened. Add the broth and shredded meat, and simmer for 5 minutes. Taste and add more salt if needed. You can cool and chill it at this stage.

If serving immediately, add the noodles and cook for a final minute, then stand off the heat for a minute to finish cooking. Ladle into bowls, adding a squeeze of lime juice, a sprinkle of chopped parsley and a grating of parmesan.

VENISON PAPRIKASH

This is a warming stew based on the popular Hungarian dish which is usually made with chicken (and you could certainly use chicken legs in this recipe). I love making it with venison, though. It is a sustainable British meat, rich in protein and iron, with a beautifully subtle game-y flavour. Traditionally paprikash is made with Hungarian paprika and served with spaetzle (a twisted egg noodle), though this version is a bit more accessible.

500 g/1 lb. 2 oz. diced venison
2 tbsp olive oil, plus more if needed
2 tbsp plain/all-purpose flour
1 large onion, halved and sliced
2 garlic cloves, finely chopped
1 red (bell) pepper, quartered, deseeded and sliced
100 g/3½ oz. tomatoes, diced
2 tsp sweet smoked paprika
350 ml/1½ cups chicken stock
5–6 tbsp soured cream, plus a little more to serve
salt and black pepper
chopped flat-leaf parsley, to garnish
tagliatelle, to serve

SERVES 4

TAKES 1 HOUR 15 MINUTES

Take the venison out of the fridge about 30 minutes before cooking and season all over with salt and pepper.

Heat the oil in a large sauté pan or shallow casserole/Dutch oven over a high heat. Toss the venison with the flour, then add to the pan and sear until browned all over but not cooked through. Lift out of the pan and set aside on a plate.

Lower the heat to medium-high, add a splash more oil if needed and fry the onion with a pinch of salt for a couple of minutes. Add the garlic and red pepper and cook for another 2–3 minutes, then stir in the tomatoes.

Add the paprika and stir over the heat for a minute, then add the chicken stock and return the venison and any juices to the pan. Grind over plenty of black pepper and lower to a gentle simmer. Cook, stirring occasionally, for 40–45 minutes, by which point the venison should be tender and the sauce thickened.

Turn off the heat and allow to cool for 5 minutes before stirring in the soured cream and season to taste. Reheat gently and serve with tagliatelle, topped with a sprinkle of chopped parsley and an extra swirl of soured cream.

CHICKEN, SHIITAKE & KIMCHI STEW

Inspired by a classic Korean dish, this one-pot stew is loaded with flavour. It is exactly the kind of dish I turn to when I'm feeling under the weather, or make for other people when they need some soothing, nutritious food in their lives. It can be prepared up to 48 hours in advance, will sit in the fridge for 2–3 days and freezes well too.

about 700 g/1 lb. 9 oz. chicken thigh fillets
2 tbsp gochujang paste
2 tbsp vegetable or sunflower oil
1 large onion, halved and thinly sliced
150 g/5½ oz. shiitake mushrooms, sliced
500 ml/2 cups chicken stock
2 garlic cloves, crushed or finely grated
2 tsp fish sauce
250 g/9 oz. kimchi (I like Vadasz)
1 tbsp soy sauce
1 tsp toasted sesame oil
salt
1 tsp maple syrup (optional)

TO SERVE
steamed rice
thinly sliced salad onions or spring onions/scallions
toasted sesame seeds

SERVES 4

TAKES 45 MINUTES

Cut the chicken into 3–4-cm/1¼–1½-inch chunks and toss with the gochujang paste and a pinch of salt. Set aside for 30 minutes if you have the time.

Heat the oil in a large casserole/Dutch oven over a high heat. Add the chicken and fry for 7–8 minutes, turning regularly, until browned in places. Add the onion and fry, stirring regularly, for another 5 minutes, then add the mushrooms and fry for another 3–4 minutes.

Add the stock, garlic, fish sauce and kimchi and simmer for 20–25 minutes until the chicken is cooked through. Stir in the soy sauce and sesame oil. You may want to add a teaspoon of maple syrup, too, to round out the flavour.

Serve with steamed rice, topping with sliced salad onions and sesame seeds.

CHICKEN & AUBERGINE RAGÙ

This is something I like to make in early autumn/fall when aubergines are still in season and we're not quite ready for the rich ragùs of winter – I like to think of it as a lighter Bolognese.

600 g/1¼ lb. bone-in, skin-on chicken thighs
3 tbsp olive oil
1 onion, finely diced
1 large carrot, grated
1 celery stalk/rib, finely chopped
1 large garlic clove, finely chopped
175 ml/¾ cup white wine
400-g/14-oz. can chopped tomatoes
500 ml/2 cups chicken stock
4 thyme sprigs
2 aubergines/eggplants, chopped into 3-cm/1¼-inch chunks
salt and black pepper
pasta or polenta, to serve

SERVES 4–6

TAKES 1 HOUR 15 MINUTES

Preheat the oven to 200°C/180°C fan/400°F/Gas 6; arrange two shelves in the oven.

Heat 1 tablespoon oil in a large ovenproof sauté pan or casserole/Dutch oven over a medium high heat. Add the chicken thighs, skin-side down, and fry for about 8 minutes until browned. Lift out of the pan and set aside on a plate.

Add the onion, carrot, celery and garlic to the pan with a large pinch of salt and fry for 8–10 minutes until soft and turning golden. Add the wine and bubble for a couple of minutes, then tip in the tomatoes and stock. Scatter over the thyme and nestle the chicken thighs back into the pan, skin-side up. Bring to a simmer and grind over some black pepper.

Meanwhile, toss the aubergine chunks with the remaining 2 tablespoons oil, season well and scatter over a large roasting tray. Place the tray of aubergine on the upper shelf of the oven and the chicken on the lower shelf. Roast both for about 50 minutes, stirring the aubergine every 15 minutes or so. It's ready when the aubergine is soft and golden and the chicken is nicely browned and the sauce has reduced. Cool both for at least 15 minutes (or cool completely).

When the chicken is cool enough to handle, remove from the sauce. Peel off the skin and shred. Pull the meat from the bones and shred. Return the meat and skin to the sauce, add the aubergine and stir together. Serve with pasta or on polenta.

COCONUT SQUASH & BLACK BEANS

About 10 years ago I took some cooking lessons from a wonderful lady called Prem in Sri Lanka that really stuck with me. Among many other dishes, she taught me how to make a pumpkin curry, of which this is a variation. You can find curry leaves in most major supermarkets now and they add a slightly savoury-citrus note that is quite delicious (leftover leaves will keep well in the freezer).

400-g/14 oz. butternut squash (cut into 2.5-cm/1-inch cubes)
2 tbsp vegetable oil
1 small onion, finely chopped
2 garlic cloves, finely chopped
1 tsp finely chopped fresh root ginger
4–5 fresh curry leaves (optional)
1 tsp mild curry powder
1/2 tsp ground turmeric
1/2 tsp ground cumin
small cinnamon stick
1/2 tsp salt, plus extra to season
400-g/14-oz. can coconut milk
240 g/1 1/4 cups cooked black beans, drained and rinsed if from a can or jar
1 lime, juice
black pepper
coriander/cilantro leaves, to garnish
steamed rice, to serve

SERVES 4

TAKES 40 MINUTES

Preheat the oven to 220°C/200°C fan/425°F/Gas 7.

Toss the squash with 1 tablespoon oil and spread over a large baking tray. Season with salt and roast for 20–30 minutes, or until golden and tender.

Meanwhile, heat the remaining 1 tablespoon oil in a large saucepan or sauté pan over a medium-high heat. Fry the onion for a couple of minutes, then add the garlic and ginger and fry for another 2 minutes.

Add the curry leaves, spices, salt and a good grind of black pepper. Fry for a minute or two until fragrant, then pour in the coconut milk and stir to combine. Add the black beans and simmer everything gently for 10 minutes.

Stir in the roasted squash and simmer for a final couple of minutes. Squeeze in the lime juice and check the seasoning, adding more salt if needed. Sprinkle over some chopped coriander leaves and serve with steamed rice.

LEMONY RED LENTIL SOUP WITH CARAMELIZED ONIONS

It takes about 20 minutes for the onions to caramelize, so I always get them on first and prepare the other ingredients while they're cooking. This is a soothing soup, perfect for winter nights.

2 tbsp olive oil
3 onions, halved and thinly sliced
1½ tsp salt
knob/pat of butter (optional)
2 garlic cloves, thinly sliced
1 tsp cumin seeds
250 g/1⅓ cups red split lentils
½ tsp ground cumin
½ tsp ground cinnamon
½ tsp ground turmeric
1 litre/1 quart chicken or vegetable stock
1 lemon, juice
3 tbsp Greek-style yogurt, plus extra to serve
4 eggs, boiled for 7 minutes
flat-leaf parsley or coriander/ cilantro, to garnish (optional)

SERVES 4

TAKES 55 MINUTES

Heat the oil in a large saucepan over a medium-high heat. Stir in the onions with ½ teaspoon salt and 2 tablespoons water (to help them wilt) and fry for 10 minutes. Add the butter (if using), garlic and cumin seeds and fry, stirring regularly, for another 10 minutes, until golden and caramelized.

Meanwhile rinse the red lentils in plenty of fresh water then leave to soak until ready to use. Get all of the other ingredients ready, too.

Scoop out about one third of the onions and set aside for garnish later.

Stir the remaining spices into the onions and cook for a minute, then add the drained lentils, the stock, 500 ml/ 2 cups water, remaining 1 teaspoon salt, juice of half a lemon and a good grind of black pepper. Simmer for 25 minutes, or until the lentils are soft and breaking apart. Check the seasoning and add the remaining lemon juice.

Take the soup off the heat and stir in the yogurt. Serve in bowls topped with the caramelized onions, extra yogurt and a halved, jammy egg. Flat-leaf parsley or coriander leaves make a nice addition, too.

INDEX

ACKNOWLEDGMENTS

A cookbook is the culmination of a lot of hard work by a lot of people, and I am so grateful for the very talented team behind this one. I may have created the recipes, but there are many others who brought them to life.

A heartfelt thank you to Julia Charles at Ryland, Peters & Small. This is the book that I have wanted to write for many years, and I am so grateful to you for allowing me the opportunity. Also, huge thanks to Toni Kay for your thoughtful, considered design and great company on shoots. And to Leslie Harrington, Abi Waters and Yvonne Doolan. Once again, it has been such a pleasure to work with the entire team at RPS.

Carolyn Barber – I loved our shoots. You exude such warmth and creativity, and you were the perfect person to make these recipes look their best. It was a joy to work with you and your gorgeous girls, Rosie and Madeleine.

Kathy Kordalis – You make everything look so effortlessly beautiful! You are such a talent and it was so lovely to work with you again after so many years.

Hannah Wilkinson – Once again, your props were spot on. Thank you so much for knowing how to make the food look so good.

Sadie Albuquerque, Lydia Mecklenburgh and Maisie Asbridge – you are all superstars! Thank you so much for all your hard work on this book.

Tom – I think you enjoyed your role as chief taster on this book more than any other, so really you should be thanking me! Seriously, though, thank you as always for your bottomless appetite, continued support and for steaming through the never-ending piles of washing up I create.

Maya – my gorgeous girl. I look forward to cooking for you for the rest of my life.